Dedicated to

Motilal Verma, our grandfather

Surindra Nath Pandey, the great revolutionary

Kultar Singh

And

All unsung Heroes of

Indian Freedom Struggle

MY WORD

Reading books has been a passion for me. Early at the age of ten, I happened to read *Sansmratiyan*, written by late Shiv Verma, a great revolutionary, who was awarded life imprisonment in the famous Lahore Conspiracy Case. This book enthused me to explore further about the lives of the great patriots, who dared all sufferings and finally the gallows viz. Bhagat Singh, Rajguru and Sukhdev.

My grandfather, Shri Motilal Verma, was a great patriot and freedom fighter. He was jailed twice – once during the '*Namak Satyagrah* in 1931 and next during the 'Quit India Movement' in 1942. The British Government confiscated all his property, making him a destitute. But he continued his struggle, working as an underpaid *Munshi* and managed to buy back the two hundred year old ancestral house. The house is still there in Katni, a city in Madhya Pradesh. Dr. Rajendra Prasad, who later became the first President of India, had visited this house in 1935. Though my Baba was a Gandhian, he never hesitated in extending support to the revolutionaries.

He had met the great revolutionary Chandra Shekhar Azad twice. He provided a safe passage to Azad from Katni to Jhansi in 1928-29. Azad, at that time, remained underground and moved to different places to avoid arrest by the British rulers. My Baba's another meeting with Azad was on the banks of holy river Ganga while he was practising shooting with his Mouser, aiming at the fishes frolicking in water.

Being issueless, my Baba adopted his nephew, my father, Shri Koushal Kishor Verma as his inheritor. The moving tales narrated by him filled my heart with immense respect for these selfless sons of the nation.

Later in 1994, I had the luck to meet Shri Surendra Nath Pandey, a colleague of Chandra Shekhar Azad, Bhagat Singh and Rajguru and one of the prime accused in the historical Kakori and Lahore Conspiracy Cases. He was quite old and debilitated, but still retained clear recollections of his revolutionary career. The discussions with him stimulated me further to gain more insight into the life of these great men and disseminate the knowledge to all, by putting my observations in writing.

I started collecting all available literature on the revolutionaries; I visited National Archives, New Delhi several times and managed to procure copies of various rare documents. The National Archives is a treasure house of Indian history and barely 10% of the knowledge available in the records has reached us. Here, I would like to commend the British, that despite having the opportunity to destroy all records at the time of leaving India in 1947, they maintained their integrity and honesty towards the history and did not tamper with the records, leaving them for an impartial scrutiny by the future generations. Though many of the files relating to British India have been preserved at British India library, London, but most rare files are still available at the National Archives. I am deeply indebted to Shri J.K. Jain, ex-*Rajya Sabha* M.P., Shahdol for his cooperation in getting me the copies of important documents like papers relating to the trial of Lahore Conspiracy Case, judgments and documents pertaining to Government of India, Punjab Government and Jail etc. between the years 1928 to 1930, from the National Archives.

In Lucknow, a memorial and Freedom Fighters Research Institute, has been established at the house of Durgadevi Vohra (popularly known as Durga *Bhabhi*), wife of Bhagwati Charan Vohra, both being great revolutionaries. I visited the facility several times to gather invaluable information from the rare books. Puja Saxena, the then Librarian, deserves my special thanks for her help.

In May 2003, I happened to meet Sardar Kultar Singh, Bhagat Singh's brother and a revolutionary himself, of Saharanpur (U.P). It was really an honour to bow before such a great soul. He and his son, Kiranjeet Singh, enlightened me with highly privileged information on the great martyr. At the same time, I was fortunate enough to visit Bhagat Singh's ancestral village, Khatkarkalan, in Jullundur district (Punjab). I was so moved at the sight of his personal belongings at Shaheed Bhagat Singh *Rashtriya Sangrahalaya*. My motivation made me to visit, village Badaraka, district Unnao (U.P), the ancestral village of Chandra Shekhar Azad. Khed (now called Rajguru Nagar), district Pune (Maharashtra), the birth-place of Rajguru, Shaheed Upwan at Mirzapur and Alfred Park (now called Chandra Shekhar Azad Park), Allahabad, where Azad was martyred. The visit to these centers was like a pilgrimage to me.

I visited Hussaniwala, at the International Border near Ferozepur (Punjab) to make my offerings at the memorial of Bhagat Singh, Rajguru and Sukhdev. I can not find the words to express how I felt there. I shall always treasure those moments. I took a firm resolve to pay my homage by writing a book on the eve of birth-centenary of Bhagat Singh and Rajguru. I shall always feel the distress of not having written a treatise on Bhagat Singh.

I feel it is my duty to narrate as to why and how I decided to write a book on Rajguru. There is no doubt about Bhagat Singh being the torch bearer among all the freedom fighters, and he has always retained his popularity in any era due to his towering personality and excellent communication skills. Rajguru and Sukhdev, who shared the same scaffold, do not deserve to be treated as inferiors but somehow, their contribution has not been acknowledged adequately by the historians writing on the history of freedom struggle. Jag Mohan, Bhagat Singh's nephew and an eminent writer, states that it is wrong just to celebrate the birth-centenary of Bhagat Singh alone. Mother Vidyadevi, his grandmother and Bhagat Singh's mother, always maintained that no picture could be complete by including her son only, as Bhagat Singh, Sukhdev and Rajguru lived and sacrificed themselves for their nation together. She always kept Rajguru's Sholapuri shoes and Sukhdev's *kulla* along with the personal belongings of her son.

Many authors have written books on Bhagat Singh. Mathura Prasad Thapar, brother of Sukhdev, wrote a book to preserve his memories. Unfortunately, Rajguru has not received enough attention from authors. He is only mentioned as one of the comrades of Bhagat Singh. In reality, he was a *Karmayogi*, always working selflessly and never expecting any credit or praise in return. Everybody would agree that he always longed to sacrifice himself for his nation. The desire to see his motherland free had peaked beyond fanaticism. If there was some job involving the risk to life, Rajguru was always there to volunteer in the first place. Sadly, Rajguru could not attract the attention of authors and film makers. He was even neglected in his own city and state. I was deeply aggrieved at not finding a single memorial at Khed, his birth place. This was the fact, which inspired me to dare write a book on this great martyr.

I have made a sincere effort not to show disrespect for the judicial system, while discussing the proceedings of the Lahore Conspiracy Case. The conspiracies set up and the subsequent misuse of the judicial procedures by the British, is in itself indicative of the state of judicial system during that era.

My respected father, Mr. Koushal Kishore Verma, retired District and Sessions Judge, has offered his blessings and guidance by helping me to write the paragraphs regarding the Lahore Conspiracy Case. Though, Shri Motilal Verma, Shri Surendra Nath Pandey and Sardar Kultar Singh have left this world for heavenly abode, I always feel their blessings are with me.

I am deeply indebted to Mrs. Anjana Verma, my wife, Mr. Manoj Morgode, my close associate, Mr. Ranjan Nagpure, the typist and Mr. Anil Nagpure for graphics, without whose contributions this book would never have seen the light of the day.

Anil Verma

Contents

Appendices

Martyrs' march into the history

Central Jail, Lahore
March 23, 1931

6.a.m.

The day had just broken out. The sun, as always, had arisen in the east, but its radiance today was dull. The ever present frightening silence inside the perimeter seemed to make the prisoners even more desperate. All inmates had anxiety and despair written over their ashen faces, as if some big storm was coming.

The routine got underway, though at a much slower pace. Everybody wanted to talk, express their apprehensions, but some hidden fear prevented them from doing so.

However, the scenario looked totally different in barrack number fourteen and cells near it, which housed Sardar Bhagat Singh, Rajguru and Sukhdev. They all emanated an aura of peaceful calm and good health. They were quiet, yet cheerful, free from all worries and unaffacted by what was happening around them.

This was an astonishing sight for jail authorties as everybody knew that their hanging had been scheduled at 0700 a.m. sharp on 24th March 1931, the very next day. They were to meet this tragic end for having revolted against the British rule for seeking freedom for their motherland. They had only 24 hours to live, yet showed no signs of the impending dreaded event.

12 Noon

As a way of tradition, the family members and relatives of the inmates are allowed to meet their beloved ones, a day prior to the hanging. In these last meetings, varied sentiments prevail. The communication usually is non-verbal, as words fail the relatives in these moments. Only a film of tears blurs the last glimpse of their dear ones.

The relatives of these great revolutionaries had also assembled at the gate of the jail by noon. Sardar Arjunsingh, the grandfather of Bhagat Singh, along with his son, Sardar Kishan Singh, daughter-in-law, Smt. Vidyawati, Smt. Parvati Devi, widowed mother of Rajguru along with her daughter, Smt. Ralli Devi, widowed mother of Sukhdev along with her brother-in-law and many other relatives, friends, well wishers and hundreds of others who wanted to treasure the last ever meeting with their beloved ones, with which they could live the rest of their lives.

The tyrannical authorities permitted only the parents of the prisoners to meet their sons, declining access to other relatives. The parents did not accept this and refused to have this last meeting. They were suddenly transformed into a symbol of courage and fortitude as they did not allow their tender sentiments to take over the pride of the self and the nation.

This news spread like wildfire among public and journalists, present outside. Within minutes, a sensational scene began to emerge when loud echoes of slogans praising the revolutionaries and condemning the heartless Government, from inside the jail, synchronized with those from outside. The dull atmosphere suddenly turned volatile and situation threatened to go out of control.

The brave mothers, however, correctly sensed that this situation could end into unavoidable firing and undesirable bloodshed of innocent people. They decided to sacrifice the desire to meet their sons and moved out of the jail premises. The mesmerized crowd followed them.

1 p.m.

Inside, unruffled by these happenings, Bhagat Singh was engrossed in reading revolutionary Lenin, a book gifted by his lawyer, Prannath Mehta. Mehta also went on to meet Rajguru and was equally taken aback by his relaxed and carefree attitude, even in the face of imminent death.

He remembered that Rajguru had become quiet and withdrawn, a few days before the sentence was pronounced. Everybody felt that he was nervous at the sight of imminent death and tried to lift his mood. Rajguru, then, disclosed to Shiv Verma, one of his colleagues, "Before meeting you people, every moment of the nineteen years spent by me in this world, brought a new disappointment on account of poverty and want of love and the life always appeared worse then hell. All this changed in company of you all within these last three years."

Shiv Verma had put a direct question about whether he was scared of death and Rajguru had said that "I am, like you, proud of what I have accomplished. I have come to realize this truth only after challenging death. If we are able to show even a glimpse of the freedom to our fellow nationals by sacrificing our lives, they would be able to walk on that path by themselves. This death, then, would be blessing for us."

After being awarded the death sentence, Rajguru had again become his usual self and was seen laughing at himself and others, including jail employees. Many thought that he was reacting excessively out of fear of death, but soon realized that it was the basic nonchalant attitude, which Rajguru had always maintained.

4. p.m.

Sardar Chattar Singh, a retired Army Hawaldar and now the Chief Warden of the Central Jail, Lahore was a kind hearted man, who was respected by all prisoners, including revolutionaries, to whom he extended great warmth. Today he appeared distant and stern.

Barkat, the barber, looked very depressed. He in whispers, disclosed to some prisoners the news of shifting of time of hanging. It was to take place at seven p.m. this evening, eleven hours before the scheduled time. Though the evening hanging was against the provisions of the Jail Manual, the terrified British Government could be expected to violate any rule or tradition.

Khan Bahadur Mohammed Akbar, the Senior Jailor, was no less agitated. He however, did not let anybody realize as to what was transpiring in his mind. Even then, for once his tongue did falter "Who can know what I am going through and what these boys actually mean to me."

The dutiful Jailor and staff, however, had left no stone unturned in making all necessary arrangements for this unlawful execution. The Lahore Conspiracy Case undertrials were called back from the Courts much earlier than schedule. Chattar Singh curtly ordered locking of all prisoners in hot and suffocating barracks at 4 p.m. instead of routine sunset time. The armed guards started patrolling continuously inside and outside the jail. No body was allowed to come in or move out. Curtain and blinds were drawn to stop a direct view. The jail closed in the afternoon instead of late evening.

What a mockery it was. The weary and sad looking faces of jail employees contrasted with bright and cheerful faces and proud walk of those, who knew that they had only few moments to live.

7. p.m.

Bhagat Singh, Rajguru and Sukhdev took their last bath and put on black clothes provided by the jail officials. The doctor recorded their weight and was surprised to note that all three had gained weight since last recording.

They demanded not to be handcuffed. Chattar Singh feared this could not be granted, being against the rules, but the heavy hearted Jailor consented. Everybody wished that the time would stop but this did not happen.

The lions moved out of their cages, had a good look at each other and then leaped to have a warm embrace. The smile over their faces signified the grace with which they had lived and now were welcoming the death. They, then, locked their arms, Bhagat Singh in the centre, Rajguru on his right and Sukhdev on his left side and started to march, surrounded by Jail officials and wardens. Bhagat Singh started to sing and both joined him immediately.

Dil se niklegi naa mar kar watan ki ulfat.
Meri mitti se bhi khusboo-e-watan aayegi.

(Even my ashes will emanate the fragrance of soil of my land.)

The three gallows stood erected on a big scaffold on one corner of the ground. The Deputy Commissioner, Lahore, accompanied by Jail Superintendent and government officials. An English Duputy Commissioner, stood on other corner. He looked perplexed at the sight of their free hands.

Bhagat Singh immediately noticed his concerns and turning towards him, said, "Well, Mr. Magistrate, you are fortunate to be able to see how Indian revolutionaries can embrace death with pleasure for the sake of their supreme ideal." This act of sheer bravery in the face of imminent death left everybody stunned and speechless.

They started to climb stairs and reached near the scaffold. Bhagat Singh bade good bye to both fellows. They immediately shouted "Long live Bhagat Singh (*Bhagat Singh Zindabad*)'. Bhagat Singh too joined the chorus and all three shouted aloud "Long live Our Struggle (*Inqulab Zindabad.*) The echoes filled the sky.

The signal had reached in the barracks. Prisoners from all corners started the shouts of a "Long Live Bhagat Singh (*Bhagat Singh Zindabad*). Long Live Sukhdev (*Sukhdev Zindabad*), Long Live Rajguru (*Rajguru Zindabad*), Long Live Our Struggle (Inquilab Zindabad), down with the imperialism (*Samrajyavaad Murdabad)*". The noise was deafening.

The crowd outside also received the message of the imminent and inevitable and became turbulent. Sardar Kishan Singh was addressing a huge rally near Mori Gate, a short distance away from jail. Pandit K. Santanam, Manager of the Laxmi Insurance Company, broke this heart breaking news to him. His grace and courage was unaffected by the sadness of the moment and he continued his speech with great composure, so that the crowd could remain in control.

On being asked about their last wish, Bhagat Singh asked for leave of two minutes. On being granted, they once again shouted "Down with imperialism, down with Union Jack, *Inquilab Zindabad* and finally, *Vande Mataram.*" They had a look at each other for the final time as if reminding each other to keep company in the other world too and kissed the ropes.

The hangmen, with trembling hands, tied their hands and feet and covered the faces with the black masks. They were made to stand on the trapdoors on the platform and ropes were looped round their necks. The knots were positioned below the chins.

The Magistrate looked at his watch: 7.33 p.m. and raised his hand.

Bolts were drawn, the trapdoors jerked open. The bodies shot downwards and then stopped abruptly. There was sudden jerking of head, followed by violent convulsions of the body. In the twilight of the setting sun, the moving shadows looked most scary. The lives ebbed out within moments and bodies became limp. They were released and placed on the ground. The doctor examined the bodies and pronounced them dead. The martyrs were on the path to immortality.

The history had been written.

A troubled childhood

Maharashtra, the land of great warrior, Chhatrapati Shivajee and particularly Pune, the city of Peshawas, has produced many gallant fighters, including Chaphekar brothers, Mahadev Ranade and Bal Gangadhar Lokmanya Tilak.

Chakan, a small village near Pune, had once served as the capital of the great kingdom established by Shivajee. Pandit Kacheshwar Bramhe, a Deshastha Brahmin and the local priest, was respected by all classes of people for his wisdom and miraculous achievements. He was a disciple of Saint Tukaram and established a temple of Lord Vishnu, which exists even today. According to folklore, he was in possession of mystique virtues and once, his continuous chanting for three days brought heavy showers of rain in the vicinity of Chakan and nearby 84 villages facing severe draught, after many priests from Satara had failed. Later, his descendants also started worshipping him.

Chhatrapati Shahuji, the grandson of Shivajee, was having disputes with Tarabai over inheritance matters. During his administrative visits, he happened to meet Panditji as teacher and offering him a gift of village Khed and three other villages. He also bestowed him with the honorific title *Rajguru* (The Royal Teacher), a title adopted as surname by his descendants. Panditji shifted to Khed but declined the offer of other three villages.

Khed, closely related to Peshawas, was located on the banks of river *Bheema*, 40 kilometers to the north of Pune. It was a famous pilgrimage centre, called *Khetaka* in past and got mention even in *Skanda Purana*. History tells us that it was the location of the great battle between Tarabai and Dilawar Khan. Holy shrines of Aalandi and Bheema Shankar and Mastani's Palace are still present in its outskirts. About 30 years ago, the place was renamed as Rajguru Nagar by the Government of Maharashtra to honour the great martyr. This also is the site of the International Airport of Pune.

His descendant, Narain, had a son Harinarain, who had two wives. From his first wife, he had a son, Waman and Five daughters. His second wife, Parvati Devi gave birth to two sons, Dinkar and Shivram, and three daughters, namely, Chandrabhaga, Warini and Godawari. It was their second son, Shivram Hari Rajguru (in Maharashtrian culture, the name of father is inserted between name and surname), who won greatest laurels for his family by sacrificing his life for the nation at a very young age of 23.

Rajguru was born, about 101 years ago, on Monday, the 24th August, 1908 (*Triyodashi* of *Shravan* month of year 1830 according to Hindu Calendar) in village Khed. By way of coincidence, Khudiram Bose (born 3rd December 1889), the great revolutionary, was hanged in the year 1908 only, thus sacrificing his life for the freedom of the nation at an even younger age of 19 years. Was it the unsatisfied soul of Khudiram Bose, which reincarnated itself to finish the remaining job?

Once respected by the royal family, the family, faced severe financial crisis. His father died of prolonged sickness when he was only six years old. The responsibility of maintaining the family befell on the young shoulders of elder brother. Dinkar was a student of tenth class at that time. He soon joined government service in the revenue department in Pune.

There is an interesting story related to his childhood. A bridge, being built on river *Bheema*, was repeatedly collapsing despite all efforts. The rumours of making sacrifices of young children to please Gods worried the parents about the security of their beloved ones. His mother was also anxious about his safety. One day, she noticed a monk staring at her son and promptly expressed her annoyance. The monk smilingly said, "Mother, Your son is not an ordinary man, in reality he is a descendant from *Lord Vishwanath* of Kashi. These incarnations occur only to eliminate the evil forces. Therefore, your son is destined to earn a lot of fame."

The simple hearted mother believed the words and corelated the prophesy with the fact that the child was named Shivram as he was born on Monday of the *Shravana* month (a month dedicated to worshipping of Lord Shiva). His horoscope also predicted a promising future and great fame. She decided not to call her son by name and started addressing him as 'Bapu Saheb'. Since then till his death she never objected to any of his deeds and her absolute faith in him served to make Rajguru even stronger. Rajguru was also deeply attached to his mother and always helped her in household works.

He was a naughty and easily irritable child. He used to take good care of marigold plants in his garden. Plucking of only one *Jhendu* (Marigold) flower for worship by a neighbour irritated him so much that he uprooted all the plants and placed them before her.

He received his primary education in a Marathi Primary School in the village Khed. Though having a wavering concentration, the child showed remarkable learning skills and family members decided to make him adept in Sanskrit. The forecast of having a bright future assured of fame and wealth further boosted their hopes, though nobody could predict that he was destined to receive the highest honour of achieving martyrdom.

He later shifted to Pune to study at New English High School at *Nana ka Bada*. On vacations, he used to go back to his native place as he liked the natural beauty and culture of village Khed very much. The family members, specially his brother, Dinkar, was insistent on learning English as it paved the way to higher eduction and good government job. Rajguru however, regarded English as a language of lowborns and used to argue with his brother as he did not want to serve under the British. Dinkar, finally, used to silence him by asking what else he intended to achieve by declining to do government service.

Once Jagatguru Shankaracharya *(Jagatguru means teacher of the world*) happened to visit Khed and stayed at the the Lord *Vishnu* Temple, built by Shivram's ancestors. Shivram was mesmerized by the sage's brilliance and eloquence. Shivram became his ardent follower and devoted himself in the sage's service. He even observed a long fast of five days without food or water to cleanse his body and soul and develop his intelligence and stamina. This strong will was reflected in long fasts observed twice by him during his detention in the Lahore jail. His demand to go with the great teacher was, however, turned down by his mother and brother. This annoyed him momentarily but he forgot this episode after few days.

Another great soul, who influenced the tender mind of the child, was Lokmanya Bal Gangadhar Tilak. The tales of great patriot's struggle for self-rule had already inspired the youth of the nation. Shivram heard his speech sitting in the first row during the great leader's visit at Khed. Later, at the residence of Shankar Rao Dixit, Shivram, a student of class third, insisted upon seeing the great man once. He was ridiculed but he boldly and confidently, without paying attention to the distracters, walked inside Tilak's room and touched his feet. Tilak fondled the child with affection, garlanded him and spoke, "The goal of self-rule will definitely be achieved with the courage and boldness of boys like Shivram." His brother, again, did not like this. He threw away the garland and curtly ordered his younger brother to concentrate on studies rather than follow the wild dreams of achieving independence shown by these so-called big leaders. This callous attitude hurt Shivram and his mother very deeply but they were helpless.

The flame of deep hatred against the British had, however, been ignited in his tender heart. He always remembered with bitterness the sight of disdainful and contemptuous look on the face of a British Officer, who was being paid respect by the simple hearted villagers. He once felt highly enraged when he saw a poor farmer being beaten mercilessly as his bullock cart had crossed paths with the motor car of a Britisher.

The year 1919 marked a turning point in the history of freedom struggle. The incident of mass massacre of thousands of innocent Indians at Jaliyan Wala Bagh dented his heart deeply and strengthened his resolve to participate actively in the struggle. This era was one of the turning points in the history of Indian freedom struggle. Though the World War I had ended, but Pune, like all other places, was quite turbulent under the leadership of Lokmanya Tilak, Chaphekar brothers and

Mahadeo Ranade. In the Congress too, the hard liners were beginning to raise their voices. His belief in the saying *Paradheen sapanehu sukh naahi* (During captivity, even the dreams will not bring any pleasure) grew firmer.

Shivram, in his youthful zeal, decided to devote himself to the freedom struggle. He started developing physical and mental strength by vigorous exercises like wrestling, and swimming, a habit he cultivated during his childhood in *Bheema* River. He hardened himself so much that he broke a hot lamp glass between his fists. He was quiet adept with sling shot, which served to refine his accurate target practice.

Dinkar, now married, shifted to Pune along with his family. Dinkar's pro-British Government servant attitude was in absolute contrast with Shivram's nationalist zeal. With the growing frustration of the youth, the relationship, between the two worsened.

One fateful day in the year 1924, the dispute reached to such an extent that Dinkar in great anger, asked his sixteen year old brother to leave the house if he did not intend to abstain from his so-called delinquent behaviour and concentrate on studies. This provided an unexpected godsent opportunity to Rajguru to break free from family ties and indulge in service of the motherland. He immediately touched the feet of both his elders and walked out of the doors.

Voyager on unknown path

A determined Rajguru started with a dhoti, one shirt and one cap on his body with only a sum of three annas (one rupee had 16 annas) in his pocket. Out of them, two annas were borrowed from his sister Varutai. He immediately after moving out of the house, met a begger and happily gave away 8 paise from his treasure to beggar's surprise. The night was spent at Pune Railway station. Still the big question loomed large as to where to go?

He decided to go to Village Khed, his native place and started walking, crossing the wooden bridge. The hunger was satisfied by nuts purchased for half anna at village Khadki. He was excited at the prospect of meeting his childhood friends but his motivation suddenly turned weaker with the thought of a need to beg for food and subsequent insistence of the relatives for returning back to Pune. He preferred not to meet any of them and spent the night in a temple outside the village. Next morning, he resumed walking towards village Indrayani. By dusk, he had reached a village, named Varke, and found the boundary wall of a well near Maruti Temple as the resting place for the night. By now, his treasure had exhausted and he deliberately tied a stone over his abdomen to suppress the pangs of hunger.

In the morning, a ridiculous thing happened, On waking, he noticed many villages standing at a distance and wondering whether the sleeping being was a human or a ghost. A cunning local teacher made them believe that he himself had witnessed the ghost climbing up and jumping back several times in the well during the night. He also said that he could confirm it by hitting the person with a stone. If he was a human, he will cry and if he is a ghost, he will jump back into the well.

Rajguru decided to play a prank. The moment, stone was pelted; he jumped in the shadow of the well's wall and threw a stone in the well. The loud thud confirmed the villager's belief that it was indeed a ghost. The elated teacher, thereafter, convinced them to arrange for a *yagna* and a large feast to get rid of the ghost. Rajguru quietly slipped in the bushes and continued to sleep.

In the afternoon, he went straight to the teacher's residence. The *yagna* was over and feast was about to be served. On Rajguru's humble enquiry as to what was going on, the teacher proudly boasted he had enticed villagers to arrange for all this and a little later he would devour a sumptuous meal and extract a handsome reward (*dakshina*) from these foolish villagers. Small quantity of food on a platter will be left at the well for the ghost and rest will be consumed by the villagers.

Rajguru then told the teacher about the whole truth and enquired whether the teacher could make available three days ration for him. The perspiring teacher now was praying before Rajguru to keep silent, because of the fear of this exposure and subsequent repercussions. Rajguru took away all the one and quarter rupee, extracted as *dakshina* and asked the teacher to leave ample food on the village well.

Poor teacher had to comply and Rajguru got away with the food. The teacher took a sigh of relief and the villagers were also happy, getting rid of the ghost. The funny episode took care of Rajguru's worries for food for three days at least.

This luxury did not last long. On feet, he crossed the villages of Lahasase, Sangamner, Nandur and Dodi. At times, he was forced to eat tree leaves to fill his hungry stomach. A Brahmin offered him the food and *dakshina* at Dodi, which somehow kept his morale up.

Finally, after walking 130 kilometers, he arrived at the holy city of Nasik. He joined an *ashram* to quench his desire of learning sanskrit. The shrine head also arranged for getting food free of cost from *Anna Kshetra*, a place for providing free food to monks and celibates.

But this was not his abode. He had left home for serving his motherland and not for food and studies. This famous saying was driving him crazy.

Janani Janmbhumishch Swargadapi Gariyase!

(The place of mother and motherland is higher than even heaven)

He left Nasik on the fourth day of arrival and boarded a train to north. Ticketless, he spent two nights and one day with water only. He was asked by a policeman to get down at Ghoti Station. Fortunately a humane South Indian Brahmin, Station Master provided him the much needed food (he was starving for past 36 hours) and helped him board a train to Jhansi at 11 p.m.

At Jhansi, he visited the Fort to pay homage to great warrior Rani Laxmibai, another idol, for whom he had immense respect. Here he met Eknath Sadashiv Gore, who advised him to go to Kashi, where better opportunities of serving the nation as well as getting good eduction were available. Both travelled for fifteen days through Lucknow, Kanpur, Lakheempur and Prayag, selling sarees and reached Kashi at 8.p.m. on the 14th day of *Shukla Paksha of Ashada* (Hindi Calender)

Clay turns to stone

After visiting the sacred Vishwanath Temple, Rajguru spent his first night in Kashi on a *ghat*. Fortunately for him, a single paisa found on way took care of his needs of food.

Next morning, he visited *Ahilyabai Ashram* to meet Pandurang Pant Joshi, an old family friend. Joshi fixed a set of six to seven houses for getting *Madhukari* (alms in the form of cooked food, given to student or saints in the morning period). Though Kashi residents regarded this as a pious act but for Rajguru, the food acquired by begging was equivalent to poison. He started to look for ways to get food in a respectable manner.

Drastic changes began to appear in Rajguru's life style. His day started at 5.a.m. long before dawn. After morning routine activities, luxurious bath and washing of clothes in the River Ganges, he was back in his room by 6.30 a.m. Then after going for *Madhukari* in five houses at around 10.a.m. he attended classes from 12.30 to 2.p.m. After an hour's rest, he resumed with revision and home work. Six to 8.30 p.m. he took leisure strolls and then dinner. He retired to bed usually by 8.30.

During that time, many Maharashtrian laureates resided at Kashi. He received education at Sangved Sanskrit School from Ved Murthy Baba Patwardhan (for study of Vedas), Mukund Shastri Puntambekar (for study of Shastras), Ved Shastri Pathak (for study of Nyaya Shastra ie. Justice) and Ved Shastri Pendre (for Laghu Siddhant Koumudi). All teachers liked him for quick learning skills and clean presentation. (Note: Not much authentic information is available about the places used by Rajguru as residence.) Mr. Naveen Singh, a famous photographer of Varanasi, upon my insistence, made an elaborate research by visiting Ahlyaghat, Ramghat and Benaras Hindi University. He was surprised to note that the Sangved Sanskrit School, still operational at Ramghat, has retained its ancient structure of building and furniture. The observance of age old dignified tradition of teacher and disciple is reflected by tonsured students clad in *dhoti* and *kurta* receiving wisdom from their teachers. It is a matter of regret that even the teachers are not aware that Rajguru had studied in this school. The records have also been destroyed.

Later in Lahore Conspiracy Case, Puntambekar testified before the tribunal for the prosecution (PW 11) over Rajguru's linguistic skills as he had studied Sanskrit under him for two and half years and he was fluent with Dakkhini (Marathi) language. Rajguru's address in Kashi was confirmed by Syed Ahmed Shah (PW 411) by means of a postal receipt recovered from his brother's house (Ex PJK), after Rajguru's arrest, which stated - Shivram Hariram Rajguru, Patnitola, House No. 5, Benaras City.

(Note: According to Naveen, the place is likely to be Pathanitola, where a muslim family has been living for more than twenty years and again, no one is aware of its historical significance. Though Rajguru spent nearly three years at Kashi, this disregardful attitude of the authorities and people is not understandable.)

Within 15 days of his arrival, he sent a post card to his brother intimating about his stay at Kashi and ongoing eduction. This brought a great relief to his mother too. The elated brother started sending him five rupees every month and this took care of stationery and food, but expenses on school fees and room rent were yet to be met.

A teacher offered to provide free education, provision of residual food and school fees, in lieu of long list of domestic jobs Gradually, job started sucking time available for studies and a restless and frustrated Rajguru decided to give up the job as well as the studies.

Shiv Verma, in his book *Sansmratiyan* recalled the exact words spoken by Rajguru, while a prisoner in Lahore Borstal Jail in 1930: "You can not understand what a great curse poverty is and how much humiliation it brings. The whole day I used to slog like an animal just to arrange resources enough to fill my empty stomach and always ended up receiving only abuses and beatings. Even then, managing school fees was difficult."

Rajguru was forced to lead a very difficult life at Kashi. He also resorted to tuitions of younger children and even labourwork, but he had a tremendous knack of survival. Once out of helplessness and to test his stamina, he spent 21 days by only consuming bitter neem leaves, germinated wheat and water. The poverty and scarcity, at times, may serve to harden the person to such an extent, where he can shape his own destiny. Rajguru was such an example.

Rajguru was only 5 feet 6 inches tall and a lean and thin person with most ordinary looks. One fine morning, he, after bathing, was offering *ardhya* (facing eastwards bowing with folded hands offering water in respect) to Sun God, while chanting *shlokas* (hymns) from *Rigveda Samhita*. He was totally unaware that a youth of the same age, attracted by his moving ear rings, was keenly observing him. His accent made the youth believe that he might be a Maharashtrian. After bath, the youth rushed to him and, speaking Marathi, asked his name.

Rajguru startled and pleased at listening to his mother tongue replied. "*Mee* (I am) Shivram Hari Rajguru. *Tujha Naao Kya* (What is your name)?"

"*Majha naao* (My name is) Shriram Balwant Savargaonkar" The youth replied.

It was like love at first sight and both became intimate friends for life. They shared their liking for wrestling, deep hatred for British and the burning desire to serve their motherland by all means. Both started living together in the premises of Neelkanth Rao Deshpande and managed free food from Siddheshwary granary. Both of them did not like to subsist on charity and found some tuition jobs, which took care of their expenses.

After dinner, both used to visit library of Chhutkamal Charitable Hospital and discuss topics of national and social interest with other friends. (The search made by Naveen suggest, now the site is under the clutches of some powerful land grabbers.) At times, when asked about as to what he intended to accomplish in future, Rajguru used to reply:

Sukhasya Dukhasya Na Kopi Data!
Paro Dadaneeti Kabuddhi Reva!
Aham Karotiti Brishabhinanam!
Swakarm Sutragrathito hi lok!!

(It is wrong to say that pleasure and grief are given by others as no one is capable of doing so. It is only false pride to believe that I do. Every human being has to pay for his deeds.)

They also founded *Geewarn Vagvardhini Sabha* for promotion of the Sanskrit language. Only Sanskrit was allowed to be spoken during its meetings. Once, the rash comments made by a science student calling Sanskrit an extinct language and English as the only practical way of communication had infuriated Rajguru a lot.

Rajguru started developing his physical and mental strength in a planned manner. He learnt wrestling and combat at *Bharat Seva Mandal* under Mr. Kudate. Another teacher, Mr. Deshmukh, taught him archery and he turned out to be a very good shooter. Due to this, later, he was regarded as the second best shooter after Azad among the revolutionaries and Lahore Case Tribunal in their verdict had also acknowledged his skills.

In academics too, in the year 1926, he showed good progress by passing *Madhyama* in *Tark Shastra* (the science of logic), an equlvalent in intermediate examination. He had learnt *Laghu Siddantha Koumudi* by heart.

During a month's leave, he visited Pune to meet his mother, to her great delight. He impressed everybody with his knowledge of Sanskrit. An intensive discussion in Sanskrit with a local laureate, Mahadeorao served only to surprise the audience and boost his image further.

Upon his return, he found the school closed due to apprehension of Hindu-Muslim riots but continued studies at his teacher's residence. This was communicated by him to his family members in a letter, dated April 28, 1926.

Savargaonkar, however, was making constant endeavours to join revolutionaries. He developed good relations with Baba Rao Savarkar, a brother of Veer Savarkar, who had come to Kashi with the dual purpose of treatment as well as to explore recruiting prospects.

Savargaonkar also got close to another great patriot, Munishwar Awasthy, who was co-editor of weekly *Swarajya* published from Gorkhpur (UP). He was nicknamed as "*Oont Saheb*" (Mr. Camel) because of his height and long neck. On Savargaonkar's insistence, Awasthy asked him whether he was aware of existence of an organization named Hindustan Republic Association. On receipt of a negative reply, he further enquired about the knowledge of the name of Chandra Shekhar Azad, the hero of the Kakori case.

This time the answer was in affirmative. Savargaonkar had heard Baba Saheb talking very highly of Azad. Awasthy informed that Azad was expected next day at Laxmi Kund in Kashi. An excited Savargaonkar managed to meet Azad through Baba Saheb, who ensured him of being given a befitting job, as and when an opportunity arose.

Rajguru learnt about this meeting on return and was overjoyed at the prospect of his dream coming true. He instantly expressed the desire to meet Azad but at first Savargaonkar took him to Baba Saheb, who convinced the two youths to give a firm commitment to serve their nation. They discussed current grim scenario prevalent throughout the nation and asked the youth like them to offer themselves in the service of the society and the motherland. Savarkar directed them to join *Hanuman Vyayam Prasarak Mandal* at Amravati to learn the skill of *Tantrashuddhi* (cleaning of system).

This was the turning point in Rajguru's life. He decided to sacrifice the chance of acquiring *Uttama* degree in Sanskrit as the revelation had already dawned upon him that for a revolutionary, the power of physical and mental strength was a greater need than mere linguistic skills.

Savargaonkar stayed at Kashi to develop his body further but Rajguru left for Amravati, borrowing money from Shri Prakash, a close aide of Baba Saheb.

The indoctrination

Hanuman Prasarak Mandal, Amravati is a voluntary organization, established in 1914 by Vaidya brothers, Anant Krishna and Amba Das, with the dual objective of development of physical and mental strength by promoting sports and culture as well as boosting national zeal among the youth. Famous social worker, Late Nirmala Deshpande (died, May 2008) has also been one of its Chairpersons. Even today, this organization is running many prestigious educational institutions.

Rajguru joined the summer camp for physical training, organized at Pannalal Garden and started rigorous training as his pastime. He soon acquired the degree of *Vyayam Visharad* (Master of Physical Training). At times, he indulged in many adventurous acts like roaming in dark in the forest, jumping into the well the or getting bitten by red ants etc. He learnt shooting with a gun acquired from his Rajasthani friend Lachchhumal, an inhabitant of village Hiberkhed, Tehsil Akot, and soon mastered its use. He found the gun to be a much more effective weapon than traditional bow and arrows.

His jovial nature and unbound zeal had already earned him many friends and admirers. He also came in contact with Dr. Keshav Baliram Hedgewar, founder of *Rashtriya Swayam Sevak Sangha* in the year 1925. He also developed close friendship with Gyaneshwar Sadashiv

Deshpande during his one year stay at Amravati. *Hanuman Prasarak Mandal* named one of its boys hostels as 'Rajguru Hostel' to commemorate the loving memory of the departed martyr, who at one time studied there.

He had already become a good wrestler and soon found the job as a gymnasium instructor. He won a lot of fame by defeating two wrestlers from Iran, who were three times heavier than him.

Rajguru, in a letter written to his mother, made his intentions clear about his joining the freedom struggle. His letter stated. "You have two sons, but one of your sons wants to serve the motherland, the mother of all mothers. I will leave Amravati soon and do not wish to come back. Do not feel aggrieved, rather by accepting my request you will bring solace to my mind. From now onwards, please remember you have only one son, Dinkar" The mother could do nothing but to yield.

It is also mentioned at places that Rajguru had also communicated this desire in person to his mother in Pune, while at Amravati.

Rajguru left Amravati and started journeying to Kashi via Pune, Nagpur and Bankhogal (Karnataka). At Bankhogal, he trained the youth from *Hindustan Seva Dal,* an organization founded by Dr. Hardikar, in the art of unarmed combat.

In the meantime, Savargaonkar, though sorely missing his friend, was progressing well on the path of struggle. Azad instructed him to arrange funds and armaments from his resources. He managed to get two German revolvers and 50 cartridges from Hyderabad, by borrowing Rs. 150 from his brother, residing in village. He showed adequate skills in procurement and smuggling of the weapons from Hyderabad to Kashi.

Savargaonkar, then, requested Azad to involve him in the operation to get Kakori Case accused released. Azad entrusted him with the job of shooting Jitendra Nath Banerjee, Superintendent of Police in Varanasi, who was responsible for getting the accused in Kakori Case punished.

On the evening of 13th January 1928, at the turning of Vishweshwar Street, Banerjee was sighted by Savargaonkar leaving home for evening rituals. Savargaonkar, in the disguise of a Pandit, fired two bullets at him and quickly dissolved in the crowd. Banerjee, however, had a narrow escape as the hurriedly aimed shots misfired and ended up with only one wound in his thigh.

A liberated Rajguru reached back Kashi, where he was soon to meet the persons, who were to shape his destiny. He got the job of Drill Master in Benaras Municipality owned High School, located in the huge garden of Raja Motichandra Palace, near Alipore station and established a private gymnasium there.

Similarity can be observed in the revolutionary carrier of both Rajguru and Azad, having roots at Kashi. Azad came to Kashi after leaving his house at a tender age of fifteen years, to study Sanskrit and got asylum in a religious establishment. He was baptized on the path of revolution, after getting a punishment of fifteen whips for shouting nationalistic slogans. Rajguru, at the same age, left his house to study Sanskrit at Kashi, got asylum in a shrine and finally started his journey to martyrdom here.

On listening to Savargaonkar's adventures, his youthful zeal started provoking him to accomplish heroic deeds. The authors are divided over as to how Rajguru earned the indoctrination. According to some Marathi laureates, he met Baba Rao Savarkar through Savargaonkar, who entrusted him with certain tasks. During execution of some task, he had met Azad at Kashi. Vaishampayan and Shiv Verma, both colleagues of Rajguru, however, narrated a different legend. According to them, a coincidence brought Rajguru in contact with Vaishampayan. Vaishampayan, after receiving Azad's approval, arranged a meeting between the two at Kanpur. This appears to be more authentic as it is narrated by the persons, who worked with Azad as well as Rajguru during that period.

The stars were beginnings to have a favourable turn for an enthusiastic Rajguru. Vaishampayan, at that time, was working as head clerk in the office of Jhansi, but in reality, was an under-cover revolutionary and a close aide of Azad. He, upon Azad's instruction, had come to Kashi to find new recruits and strengthen the communication links. One day, in a garden, when he was sitting on a bench and contemplating in peace, a British, with the intent to occupy that seat, tried to manhandle him. Coincidentally, Rajguru happened to be there and could not tolerate the unpleasant sight of a British mercilessly humiliating an innocent fellow Indian. He, in great rage, gave the British a good beating and fled away with Vaishampayan.

Vaishampayan thanked him and soon both started discussing the British atrocities. Rajguru outrightly advocated the use of guns and bombs to have British expelled from the country, as they could never understand the polite language of peace and non-violence. Vaishampayan was deeply influenced by his self-confidence, determination and love for the nation. He informed Rajguru that he also belonged to Maharashtra and was making efforts for gaining entry in some revolutionary group, while staying at Kanpur. Rajguru informed him that he too held similar views and was keen to join such group, if Vaishampayan found any. Vaishampayan promised to create some opportunities for him.

Vaishampayan, on his return to Jhansi, informed about this dashing youth to Azad. Azad, at that time, was busy in planning to extend the Indian Democratic Organization to all states of the country. On the recommendation of Vaishampayan, Azad contemplated that the youth deserved a chance and consented for an interview at Kanpur to test Rajguru's mettle.

Few days later, Rajguru was escorted to Kanpur by Vaishampayan. The meeting took place and Rajguru was subjected to intense, yet most interesting, interrogation;

Azad: "So, you wish to join revolutionaries."

Rajguru: "Yes, I do and have been making constant efforts in this direction."

Azad: "Despite knowing that it could culminate into a bullet-ridden body, hanging or exile."

Rajguru: "Yes, I am aware but do not feel intimidated by these meaningless results."

Azad: "Your assets?"

Rajguru: "I consider myself physically strong and trained enough for unarmed combat and am quite willing for any such job any time. Though I have not practiced shooting much but feel confident about combating with a lathi or a knief. I am also ready to kill anybody or risk my life for the supreme cause. I can survive without food for three to four days and on tree leaves for few more days. I can withstand severe torture."

Azad: "And your weaknesses?"

Rajguru was honest: "Sleepiness. I, at times, may land into deep sleep, even while standing or walking."

That was enough. Azad was highly impressed by Rajguru's attitude, tremendous self-confidence and honesty and signalled his confirmation. Rajguru's joy knew no bound as his life long ambition was being fulfilled.

Azad detailed him about objectives and rules (including code signs) of the group. He was assigned the code name "Raghunath." In Lahore Conspiracy Case, he was also referred to as "M" (M stands for probably Maratha). Azad asked him to go back to Kashi and continue with the job. Azad told him that he would be called in hour of need and then he will be required to relinquish all his possessions and leave at once. Rajguru touched Azad's feet and went back.

According to legend, Azad took him and other colleagues in the woods of Khaliadhana, Orchha of Bundelkhand Kingdom for training in shooting as loud firing shots there could easily mingle inconspicuously with those fired by local Thakurs during hunting. His adeptness in shooting soon won Azad's affection and confidence to such extent that he was called specifically at Lahore for executing the assassination of Scott. He proved himself worthy of this confidence by shooting Saunders, while he was riding on a motorcycle.

In the league

In late 1927, the freedom struggle had become quite stagnant as the 'Divide and Rule' policy of British was highly successful in creating a great communal divide between Hindus and Muslims.

Hassan Nizami, a Delhi resident was creating many headaches for the society and revolutionaries, in particular. The Central Committee decided to eliminate him. The Group entrusted Shiv Verma, a student of DAV College, Kanpur with this job. Azad asked to choose one accomplice for this mission. After discussing many names, Azad, himself, recommended the name of Rajguru, the new recruit, as an accomplice. Shiv Verma was given Rajguru's address and was asked to contact him.

Like everyone, Shiv Verma too was taken for a ride by Rajguru on their first meeting. In his book, *Sansmratiyan* (Memorabilia), Verma has given an interesting narrative of what went on between the two:

As Shiv Verma had been informed about Rajguru's occupation as a school drill master, he naturally projected Rajguru appearing as a smart looking, army styled man. But, Rajguru was a unique personality by himself. In reality, Shiv Verma was taken aback at the sight of an ordinary looking 5.5 feet tall, lean and thin youth having dark complexion and bony face with sunken cheeks He appeared to be much older than his twenty years age.

The loose fitting khaki knickers, sagging half sleeved white shirt, black cap over finely cropped hairs and ear ring in only one ear added no further to the appearance and, searching and vacant looks in the eyes rather made him scary. The appearance, however, changed with the passage of time. The only thing which did never change was his intense sleeping habit.

Rajguru, at the time, was continuing his job as a drill master in the High School as well as training the youth in the use of *Lathi*, *gada* and other indigenous weapons in a gymnasium. The gymnasia of that era played an important role in freedom struggle by arousing awareness about national integrity and also served as nursery for revolutionaries. Rajguru also shared the similar notion and took a lot of interest in educating the youth.

Shiv Verma did not find Rajguru at the school and was directed towards gymnasium. On reaching the gymnasium, Shiv Verma found a person, looking like a labourer, cleaning and arranging the gymnasium. Verma took him for a menial and enquired about Rajguru.

Rajguru snarled in reply, "Why do you want to meet him?"

Verma: "I can tell the purpose of my visit to him only."

Rajguru: "I am Rajguru. Now you tell me the purpose of your visit."

A startled Shiv Verma could not believe this but on exchanging the codes, the doubts cleared. Rajguru locked the room and took him to a secluded area near Moti Jheel. He still did not show any warmth upon meeting a colleague for the first time. The expressionless looks, however, changed to smile only when Verma told him about the upcoming opportunity. He said, "Fine. At last the party finds me of some use. Now tell me when and where I am supposed to be present."

On getting Rajguru's instant approval, Verma asked him to take one month leave and reach his room in Science block, DAV College at Kanpur.

Rajguru, in great enthusiasm, reached there within seven days only. Shiv Verma was occupying a room in the science block, due to shortage of the rooms in the hostel.

The DAV College, Kanpur and its hostels served as the national headquarters for conducting revolutionary activities and witnessed the nurturing of great patriots like Chandra Shekhar Azad, Bhagat Singh, Batukeshwar Dutt, Shiv Verma, Ajay Ghosh, Surendranath Pandey, Mahaveer Singh and many others.

As the second gun was not arranged by that time, Rajguru was forced to stay with Shiv Verma for fifteen days. He spent those days sleeping heavily on an extra cot in Verma's room. During this period, he got up only for morning rituals and meals. The curiosity of Verma's friends and wittiness of Rajguru, whenever combined, produced great humorous incidents.

Once a friend asked, "Are you paid for sleeping?"

Rajguru replied, "Not so, Actually I might get a night shift job through a friend. Since I would not have time to sleep at that time. I wish to avail this luxury now."

Another friend teased, "I think, you might be preparing for some sleeping competition."

Rajguru was equal to the task, "I have no equal. Where does the question of rivalry arise?"

A third friend darted another sparkle, "What if we rename you as Neendram Rajguru instead of Shivram Rajguru?"

Rajguru was never to give up, "One of my ancestors earned the title of Rajguru by virtue of his wisdom. If I am to be renamed, my choice will be Shivram Neendguru."

The message was clear, No body disturbed him after this and he continued to enjoy sleep like *Kumbhakarna*.

First step towards revolution

Shiv Verma and Rajguru, after fifteen days, left Kanpur for Delhi with only one gun. Delhi was in its early phases of development. They stayed in an inn and soon were on the job of watching their target, Hassan Nizam.

Next day, Rajguru stayed in the room due to headache while Verma alone left for observation. Upon his return at nine at night, Verma found Rajguru, covered with blanket yet shivering, standing on the road outside the inn. He ran towards Verma on sighting him and blurted out, "This place is not good. Let us move to another inn."

Verma wanted to learn as to what had transpired but Rajguru was adamant on leaving the place first. They finally moved to third class waiting hall of Railway Station. Lying down side by side, Rajguru shyly told that the inn was being managed by goons. On futher exploration, a funny story emerged:

After he was back from evening meals, an elderly gentleman came to the room and asked Rajguru whether he was comfortable or not, Rajguru took him to be a fellow visitor and replied in negative.

He asked Rajguru not to feel shy and promised to arrange anything whatever his guest wished, within minutes. Rajguru failed to understand the message and maintained that he did not need any thing.

The elderly man was not to give up so soon. He very politely said. "I understand your hesitation, no problem. I will ask my son, an equivalent of your age. You will probably be frank with him."

A young male followed soon and, after exchanging greetings, started talking to Rajguru.

Young male: "Where is your friend?"

Rajguru: "He is out for some work and should be back by 10.30 p.m."

Young man: "We could arrange those things here only. There was indeed no need to move out in this chilly night."

Rajguru: "No, the job was too special."

Young man: "Then, he must have gone to some particular place. Try us once and you would never think of any other facility. But brother, why you opted not to accompany him?"

Rajguru: "I was feeling sick and my head was heavy."

Young man: "O.K. I will arrange for it too."

Rajguru: "How?"

Young man: "I am calling three females who will take care of your headache. You can pick anyone you like. She will manage to get you a soothing gentle massage and sound sleep."

Rajguru was dumb-founded. Now he realized that he was actually dealing with pimps. He still signalled his negation which the pimp interpreted as otherwise and soon returned with three beautiful women.

That was enough. Rajguru picked up his baggage and ran like a wild horse, avoiding the vulgar invitations by the females.

Frash Khana: Encounter between Rajguru and police took place

The Office of Police Suprentendant in Lahore where Saunders was shot on 17th Dec, 1928

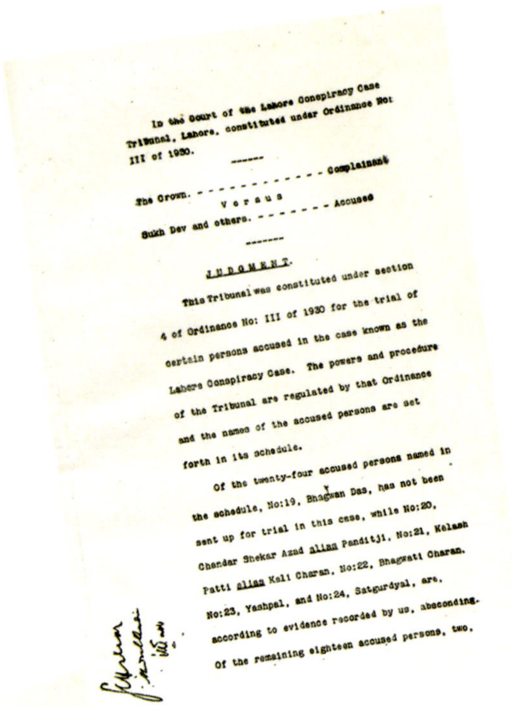

In the Court of the Lahore Conspiracy Case Tribunal, Lahore, constituted under Ordinance No: III of 1930.

The Crown. - - - - - - - - - - - - - Complainant

V e r s u s

Sukh Dev and others. - - - - - - - - Accused

J U D G M E N T.

This Tribunal was constituted under section 4 of Ordinance No: III of 1930 for the trial of certain persons accused in the case known as the Lahore Conspiracy Case. The powers and procedure of the Tribunal are regulated by that Ordinance and the names of the accused persons are set forth in its schedule.

Of the twenty-four accused persons named in the schedule, No:19, Bhagwan Das, has not been sent up for trial in this case, while No:20, Chandar Shekar Azad alias Panditji, No:21, Kelash Patti alias Kali Charan, No:22, Bhagwati Charan, No:23, Yashpal, and No:24, Satgurdyal, are, according to evidence recorded by us, absconding. Of the remaining eighteen accused persons, two,

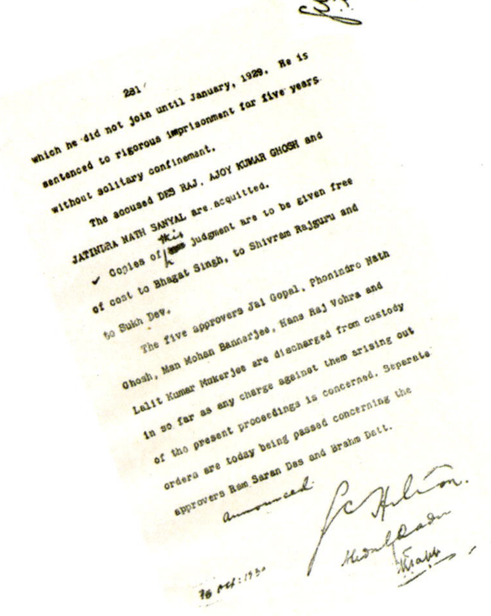

281

which he did not join until January, 1929. He is sentenced to rigorous imprisonment for five years without solitary confinement.

The accused DES RAJ, AJOY KUMAR GHOSH and JATINDRA NATH SANYAL are acquitted.

Copies of this judgment are to be given free of cost to Bhagat Singh, to Shivram Rajguru and to Sukh Dev.

The five approvers Jai Gopal, Phonindro Nath Ghosh, Man Mohan Bannerjee, Hans Raj Vohra and Lalit Kumar Mukerjee are discharged from custody in so far as any charge against them arising out of the present proceedings is concerned. Seperate orders are today being passed concerning the approvers Ram Saran Das and Brahm Datt.

announced

7 oct: 1930

The first and last page of court's verdict

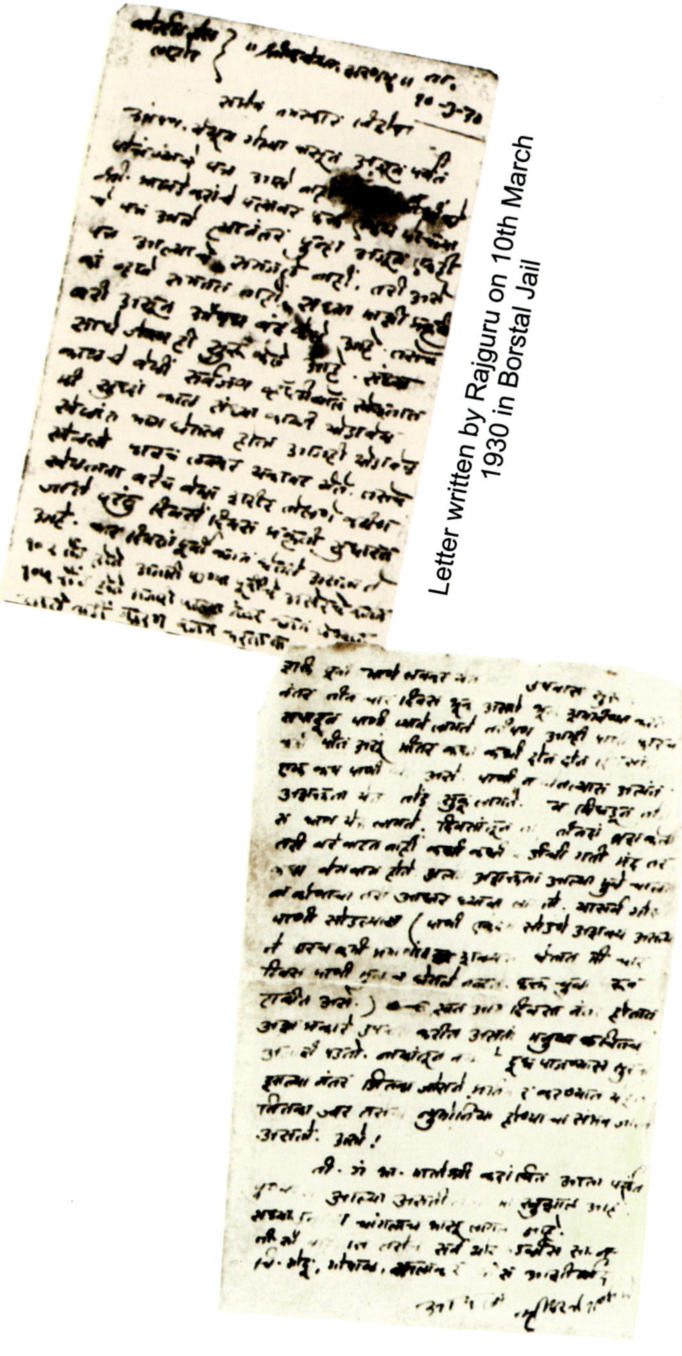

Letter written by Rajguru on 10th March 1930 in Borstal Jail

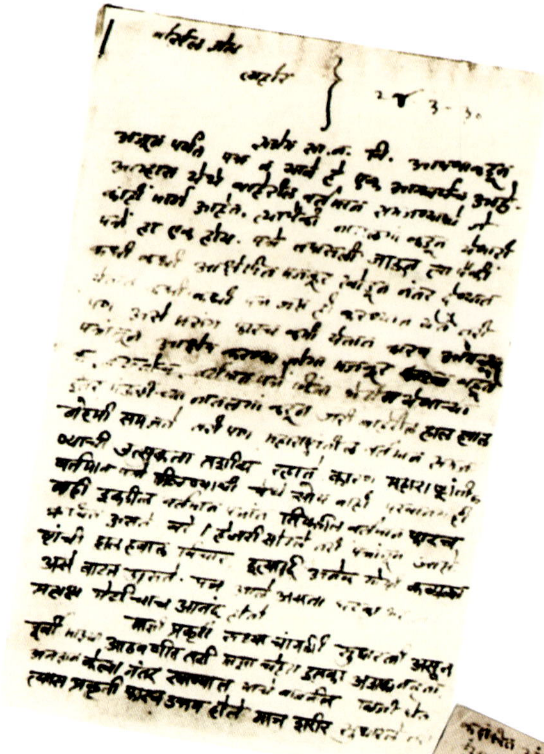

Letter written in Marathi

Letter written in Marathi on 23rd March, 1930 by Rajguru in Borstal Jail

Shiv Verma, too, had a hilarious laugh and started teasing Rajguru, "Why did you get so scared. They could not have eaten you alive."

Rajguru sheepishly replied, "I was awe-struck indeed as I sensed that they were capable of doing anything to me." After sometime, Rajguru got up and started patting his back with the words, "At least, this proves that I am smart enough to attract three beauties together." Shiv Verma pulled him back and said, "Now get inside the blanket, otherwise cold will take away all the glamour." The night, thereafter, was spent in laughter.

Rajguru started accompanying Verma for the watch. After few day's of watch they came to a conclusion that for ensuring a successful outcome of this operation, two guns were necessary in an event of a misfire or breakdown. Shiv Verma left for Lahore to arrange for the second gun, handing his gun to Rajguru. Rajguru was instructed to continue the watch and keep the gun safe.

Rajguru, in disguise, continued watch on Nizami. One day he, learnt that Nizami was likely to be alone near Madarkhana for some dinner arrangements on the night of 30th January, 1928. He decided to accomplish the job that very night only, alone, without waiting for Shiv Verma, as he was not sure when Verma would come back.

In the night, Rajguru saw Nizami's car coming from a distance. He released the lock and waited. The door opened and a man walked out. The moment had arrived and he fired.

The shot was accurate. The man collapsed instantly as the bullet hit him on the chest.

He immediately dashed away and after running for three kilometers, reached railway track to Mathura. He now started walking briskly feeling more relaxed.

Suddenly there sprang lights and firing started from many directions. He immediately started crawling in a gutter to reach the nearby field. There he lay submerged in water, holding his breath. The frantic searching by police men went on in the drier area as no one could imagine that he would dare to hide in the chilly waters. The silence was broken by sounds of moving boots and voices of policemen with intermittent firing.

All sounds stopped at nearly three in the night. A shivering Rajguru came out of the water and performed some exercises to infuse some warmth in the body. His body and clothes were smeared with mud and his body had turned numb due to prolonged contact with cold water and mud. He resumed walking along the railway track and crossed two stations before reaching Hazrat Nizamuddin. He, then, boarded a train to Mathura, quietly occupying a vacant upper berth.

Luckily for him, the train stopped at the outer signal before Mathura. He alighted and took a bath in river Yamuna, left his clothes to dry in open and went into deep sleep on the sandy shores. The revolver had already been buried under the sand.

In the morning, he woke up. He bought a newspaper, with the curiosity of seeing his heroic deed in print. He was, however, in for a great shock at reading that the person shot was not Hassan Nizami, but his father-in-law. A newspaper's headline read 'Father-in-Law of Hassan Nizami killed' while another, mentioned 'Brother Somali shot in personal disputes'. All his enthusiasm vanished immediately and he turned sore.

The actual culprit was missed and an innocent man was killed by him.

He returned to Kanpur with a sense of deep guilt and frustration. On reaching back, he started crying before Shiv Verma for his failure and said, "Prabhat (code name for Shiv Verma. I feel guilty for my haste, I sincerely offer my regret. I hope not to be expelled from the party because I failed to accomplish the task entrusted to me. I do not know what will be my future." Shiv Verma consoled him a lot and asked him not to be chicken hearted as by now Nizami must have learnt for whom the bullet was intended.

In reality too this was only a result of haste and was excusable. Later Azad too lifted him with words and a pat on his shoulders. "You cannot be expelled. You are courageous, confident, accurate in shooting and gutsy enough to shake off police trail." These words of encouragement really lifted a heavy weight from Rajguru's heart.

Though he was never tried for this murder, Rajguru always felt guilty of having killed on innocent man for the rest of his life. Anyway, he had already announced his arrival in the scene of Indian freedom struggle.

Wit has no end

Within few days after returning from Delhi, Rajguru happened to meet a jovial Sikh youth, who turned out to be his greatest friend as well as the biggest rival for the rest of their lives.

He introduced himself as "Ranjeet" and landed in Rajguru's arms as Rajguru uttered his name as Raghunath. His real name was Sardar Bhagat Singh, one of the greatest Indian revolutionaries. Sukhdev, Bhagat Singh's childhood friend, completed the trio. They became so intimate that even at the gallows, all three were hanged together.

Bhagat Singh and Rajguru were in absolute contrast to each other. Bhagat Singh, being on attractive looking educated person always commanded respect from his colleagues than his less qualified, ordinary looking colleague. Rajguru used to say that if Ranjeet said that there was water, everyone would believe him but if I said *Paani*, no one would even bother to pay attention to me.

This triggered a rivalry between the two. This, though, could never be termed as jealousy. Rather the rivalry was for being the foremost to make sacrifice for the country. Rajguru always offered himself at the first call, the intensity definitely increasing in presence of Bhagat Singh. He always pressed the leadership to be given a preference over Bhagat Singh for any job. The colleagues used to ridicule him for this but at times, this attitude created managerial problems for the leadership.

The close relationship between the two can be appreciated from the fact that when the tribunal proceedings were being initiated in the Lahore Conspiracy Case against Bhagat Singh, Rajguru had turned quite anxious as Bhagat Singh was likely to beat him on the path of sacrifice. It is said, that he deliberately exposed himself out of safety at Pune so that he could equal the scores with his beloved friend.

The rivalry, however, did not affect their intimacy and both, in tandem, performed some of the most important operations in the history of Indian freedom struggle. Not only did he become a partner of Bhagat Singh in all circumstances, but also showed total obedience to him, as Bhagat Singh was his superior in the party hierarchy. He volunteered himself to play the role of Bhagat Singh's servant quite willingly. Combination of this degree of selfless friendship and healthy competition has only few equals in the history.

Joining the group had induced a magic transformation in Rajguru's personality. The introvert and disdainful attitude, casual life style and forlorn looks became a thing of past. He had now become an open, self confident and jovial person, in the company of well educated colleagues, belonging to good families. The transformation was even more pronounced during the last days of his life. He regarded the three years spent in the group as the most precious period of his life.

Admitting this before Shiv Verma, at the fag end of his life, he had said. "I spent 19 years in this material world before meeting you people. Believe me. Prabhat, I remained oblivious to the beauty of the world. Every moment seemed to bring a new curse, a new burden over my mind and the life appeared worse then hell. These three years with you all seem to have brought a new hope and joy."

Despite all changes, Rajguru could never resist his *Kumbhakarna* like deep sleep and this handicap, sometimes, put him in deep trouble. There were, however, many comical situations too.

Once the group, to resolve the ever-present financial crisis, decided to plan a robbery on Government Treasury at Gorakhpur. Bhagat Singh, Rajguru and Shiv Verma were sent to Gorakhpur for this job. They stayed in an old shop, at a rent of Rs. five per month. They spent the whole day in watch and required the facility for only taking rest at night. They had cleaned the front room only for the use as there was lot of junk packed in the other room.

On the very first night itself, they had gone into deep sleep over a carpet on the floor. At around one at night, Shiv Verma awoke on hearing some hissing sound and suspecting presence of a snake, woke Bhagat Singh too. In torch light, both saw a hooded hissing snake by the side of Rajguru's head. Bhagat Singh pulled at Rajguru's foot and shouted. "Wake up. There is a snake by the side of your head." Rajguru merely turned around, said, "Do not disturb me" and went back to sleep again. The snake, however, escaped into the other room.

In the morning, on being told about the incident, Rajguru started complaining as to why he was not woken up immediately. Bhagat Singh and Shiv Verma could do nothing, but stare, at each other and smile.

The execution of robbery plan was looking quite a distant possibility. After few days, they all decided to leave for Kashi, The tickets were purchased well in advance in the morning. Bhagat Singh and Shiv Verma left early to meet Haldhar Bajpyee, a student of Gorakhpur Technical School and they asked Rajguru to meet near Railway Bridge.

After meeting Bajpayee, both arrived only 20 minutes before the scheduled departure of the train but Rajguru was nowhere to be found. Thinking that Rajguru might have boarded the train, they made three quick searches in all compartments but could not find Rajguru. Following the standard instructions of leaving the place immediately in the event of a companion gone missing, they had to board the train and leave Gorakhpur immediately.

Next day, after lunch, they were relaxing in the room of Jaidev Kapoor, an engineering student and local organizer. Suddenly an annoyed Rajguru appeared and started "You selfish fellows, how could you leave me alone, without money and ticket?"

Shiv Verma tried to control the situation, "This is not the case, we searched for you everywhere and could not find you. But, where were you?"

Rajguru sheepishly replied, "I was sleeping among the beggars by the side of the bridge as I thought it was the best way to utilize one hour, that I had. But, anyway, you should have woken me up."

Bhagat Singh said, "But, we thought you were apprehended by the Police."

Rajguru, now proudly removing revolver from his pocket, said, "Then what was this toy meant for."

After prolonged discussion, the matter was dropped, Later, after an explanation from Bhagat Singh,

Rajguru admitted his mistake and promised not to repeat it in future.

Rajguru had a unique quality of even ridiculing himself just to keep the atmosphere jovial. The bitter memories of deprivation of affection starting from early childhood since the loss of his father and the hardships faced by him at Kashi had vanished in the new found company.

Once he was travelling by train with Bhagat Singh to Delhi. Due to heavy rush, they could not find a place to sit. Still, a person was occupying two seats by keeping his baggage there. Rajguru, seeing this, asked Bhagat Singh to move there.

Bhagat Singh was not enthusiastic, "Why will he give us space? He is not related to us."

Rajguru was optimistic, "He will, he looks my brother."

Bhagat Singh corrected him, "he looks like my brother."

Rajguru did not seem to bother, "Do not worry about English. Don't you see he looks uglier than me. I feel that my elder is bound to give a seat."

Both started moving towards the seat. The man appeared uglier and more talkative than Rajguru by appearance. Understanding their intentions, the gentleman started lecturing the fellow passengers over the dirty habits of the Indians, "Just look at these young folks. They enter the compartment, marching like a king without difficulty. And, I poor chap, faced great hindrances in entering and had to travel standing for two stations before getting the luxury of a seat. They look capable of standing for more then six stations without getting tired.

Rajguru, sensing him to be a tough nut, decided to play a prank on this cunning person. Pointing towards his box over the seat, he politely requested, "Please put this *bhabhiji* over the upper berth and accommodate this younger brother of yours."

The gentleman turned angry at this awkward joke, "Which *Bhabhiji*? Do not talk nonsense to me."

Despite Rajguru's insistence, he refused to move the box. But, Rajguru was still persuasive. "I am addressing you as elder brother and making a request. Tell me that you consent to be my elder."

Now the gentleman turned philosophical, "We all are children of God as he had created us. Therefore every male is my brother and every female is my sister."

Rajguru darted an innocent question. "Then *bhabhiji* too should be your sister." This made everybody smile.

The gentleman, now, was stammering. "I meant, we all are created by Him."

Rajguru interrupted, "But not you and me."

The gentleman was visibly irritated. "what do you mean?"

Rajguru, pointing towards Bhagat Singh, said, "Look at him. God has created him using good material and has given good finish. He arrests everyone's attention towards him only. We are tired of keeping him away from girls, who adore him. And we poor folks! It appears that God entrusted us to some corrupt petty contractor as he does not have time for all. He probably failed to examine us before throwing us in this mortal world. If He had at least examined us, then He must have made some repairs on my roughened face and most absurd looks. It is a pity that the contractor implanted pig hairs over your scalp just to cut on the cost."

Now everybody was laughing aloud. The gentleman was now enraged. "It is a curse to sit with vagabonds like you." He, then, walked away with his baggage and the vacant seats were occupied by our heroes.

Hindustan Socialist Republican Army

Rajguru visited Pune for a few days. At that time, his nephew and childhood friend, Gangadhar was studying for matriculation Examination. Rajguru showed him the cutting of the front page news about murder of Hassan Nizami's father-in-law, published in *The Times of India*, Delhi edition, Gangadhar could not believe that his uncle had killed him. To convince him, Rajguru showed him the old clothes, false beard and revolver locked in the trunk. Still Gangadhar wondered whether a person could appear so quiet after performing an act of this magnitude. He, however, promised to remain silent on this matter on Rajguru's request.

At the same time, in Delhi the isolated and scattered revolutionary cadres were going through the process of a major structural reform. The history was almost being re-written.

A national level meeting of all organizational representatives was organized at the historical relics of Firoz Shah Tuglak Fort at Delhi on 8th and 9th September, 13 1928. The two day long deliberations were attended by nearly a dozen persons, including Sukhdev and Bhagat Singh from Punjab, Kundanlal from Rajputana, Shiv Verma, Brahma Dutt Mishra, Jaidev, Bijoy Kumar Sinha and Surendra Nath Pandey from Central Provinces and Fanindra Nath Ghosh and

Manmohan Banerjee from Bihar. Though Chandra Shekhar Azad was not able to attend the meeting, but he had already assured Bhagat Singh of obeying the majority decision. The colleagues from Bengal refused to attend the meeting despite best efforts from Shiv Verma.

The young blood had already become weary of dormant and autocratic leadership of Jai Chand (Punjab) and J.N. Sanyal (Central Provinces). The state level groups like *Anusheelan*, *Yugantar*, *Hindustan Prajatantra* Sena and Benaras Revolutionary Party were in need of urgent integration for better effectiveness. Bhagat Singh and Sukhdev were successful in convincing all delegates for unification of command in the hands of a core group. The organization was unanimously named as Hindustan Socialist Republican Army (*Hindustan Samajwadi Prajatantra Sena*).

A Central Committee was formed for streamlining the struggle. This was the apex body for making policy decisions. Sukhdev, Fanindra Nath Ghosh, Kundanlal and Shiv Verma were elected State Organizers for Punjab, Bihar, Rajputana and Central provinces respectively while Bhagat Singh and Bijoy Kumar Sinha were included as inter-state Coordinators. Setting a new trend, Chandra Shekhar Azad was elected Commander-in-Chief of the organization.

The financial status of the group was so low that many delegates found it difficult to manage to and fro fares. Once, to meet some incidental expense of only 8 to 10 rupees, Bijoy Kumar Sinha was forced to sell the return ticket of Fanindra Nath Ghosh.

Following basic policy resolutions were adopted in the meeting:

- Central Committee would be in absolute control of the weapons and finance. The weapons would be allotted to the respective state for a specific assignment only and then returned back to Central Committee after conclusion.
- Robbery should be resorted to for arranging finances. As far as possible, only Government banks, treasury or post offices would be targetted.
- The organization would deal with issues of national and social significance only. To start with, active participation in Simon Commission boycott activities must be ensured and to express intensity of public dissent, effort should be made to bomb the train carrying the members.
- Efforts seeking forcible release of Yogesh Chandra Banerjee, a Kakori Case detainee, should be made.
- Persons capable of making a bomb and training the members in its use should be recruited.

Azad agreed to comply with the decisions and started organizing the group. The headquarters was also shifted from Agra to Jhansi.

The group was facing financial crisis in the implementation of the plans. Fanindra Nath Ghosh invited Azad and Bhagat Singh to Betia (Bihar) for exploring the possibility of a robbery. Both went there prepared but after few days, they were back without results.

Kailashpati, an employee at Gorakhpur Post Office, after seeking leadership's approval, fled away with Rs. 1800/-, which served to meet incidental expenses for a few days.

It is also noteworthy that both the architects of first two operations of the newly formed group, Fanindra Nath Ghosh and Kailashpati, had turned approver in Lahore conspiracy case and inflicted great damage.

From flame to fire

The British governance system, under the cover of The Government of India Act, 1919, was mercilessly suppressing the voice of hapless Indians all over the nation. The communal riots, increasing since 1924, and labour strikes served to complicate the situation further. The recession seemed to affect farmers, labourers, middle class and capitalists equally. As a result, there was resurgence of desire to fight for freedom among the public. The British, anticipating greater resistance, were making hectic efforts to control the situation.

Under such circumstances, on 8th November 1927, The Viceroy, on behalf of the Government, announced that a high level Commission had been appointed by Stanley Baldwin, the British Prime Minister. The members would tour India and submit a report to the Government, including suggestions on the administrative reforms. The seven member Commission was headed by Sir Elsbrook John Simon, a famous London Barrister. One of the members of the Commission, Clement Attlee later became the Prime Minister of Britain at the time of independence of India. The Commission was opposed all over India, including Congress as it did not have any Indian as its member. Barring only a few moderates, everyone in India was shouting, "Simon, go back."

Pandit Jawahar Lal Nehru, later the first Prime Minister of the independent India, has written about the report. "The Commission was greeted everywhere with a singular slogan, 'Simon, go back'. Even the illiterate had learnt to shout the three English words. Every Indian felt offended by the realization that only seven fair skinned persons were deliberately chosen to give their biased and whimsical verdict over the fate of several million Indians.

The arrival of the Commission at Mumbai on 3rd February 1928 triggered nation-wide protests. The dock workers shouted anti-commission slogans and raised black flags. The Police was forced to open fire at Madras, leading to death of three persons. The resistance was intense at Calcutta too. The Commission returned back to England after finishing the first round of visit on 31st March 1928. The second round was to start in October 1928.

The morale among the revolutionaries was up under the dynamic leadership of Bhagat Singh. They, with the approval of Central Committee, had already planned to bomb the carriage carrying the members, but failed to implement it at the last moment due to paucity of funds. The Lahore Unit, however, decided to oppose the Commission's visit by organizing a strong protest demonstration under the worthy leadership of *Punjab Kesari*, Lala Lajpat Rai. The organization of the movement was entrusted to *Noujawan Bharat Sabha*, an organization erected by Bhagat Singh himself. Lalaji, too, consented to lead the demonstration.

The Commission arrived at Lahore on 30th October 1928. There was total strike in the city. A crowd of five thousands odd persons had already gathered at Lahore Railway Station, though the administration had enforced Section 144, Criminal Procedure Code, banning such gathering of protestors.

All political parties and organization had joined together under the leadership of *Noujawan Bharat Sabha*. *Shere-e-Punjab* (The Lion from Punjab) Lala Lajpat Rai was leading the protest from the front accompanied by Bhagat Singh, Sukhdev, Yashpal, Bhagwati Charan, Dhanvantari, Sardar Kishan Singh, Hansraj Bhardwaj, Dr. Gopichand Bhargava and Dr. Satyapal and many other stalwarts. Young men, in order to protect their esteemed leader, had organized themselves in a protective ring around him while holding an umbrella over his head.

The crowd began to move forward as the members of the Commission walked out of station premises. The black flags and slogans of *Inquilab zindabad*. *Angrez murdabad* and 'Simon, go back' started filling the atmosphere. The slogan *Inquilab zindabad*, coined by Bhagat Singh...., was first used on this very day. Few demonstrators also sang the couplet:

Hindustani hai hum, Hindustan hamara,
Chale jaao Simon, jahan hai desh tumhara.

(We are Indians and this land belongs to us. Go back. Simon, where you belong to.)

J.A. Scott, Superintendent of Police, Lahore, along with Saunders, his Additional S.P. and other officers was present at the station. He analyzed the situation critically and sensed that dealing with this front ring was the only way to disperse the crowd and clear the path. He ordered the lathi charge but there was hardly any impact as the crowd was back at its place almost immediately.

An infuriated Scott now let his force loose on unarmed people. Saunders, with a cane in his hands, too joined the assault. He directly attacked Lalaji, breaking his umbrella. The broken parts and cane blows resulted in severe injuries over his head, chest and left shoulder. Despite stiff resistance from youth, the assault continued for nearly half an hour. The aged lion fell down in great pain, bleeding heavily from the wounds. Youth still wanted to continue but Lalaji ordered them to call off the demonstration in protest against cruel attitude adopted by the Police. The convoy now moved to Governor house as the crowd, complying with Lalaji's directives, had dispersed.

The news about this brutal assault spread to all corners like wildfire. Lalaji undaunted by this, addressed the protest meeting held the same evening at Mori Gate at the instance of Congress. The wounded lion loudly roared, "I declare that the blows struck at me will be the last nails in the coffin of the British rule in India." Many police officers, including Neil, Deputy SP, were also present in the meeting.

Lalaji was hospitalized for the treatment of his injuries. He, after 18 days, succumbed to the injuries on 17th November, 1928. The whole nation mourned over the death of the departed leader. There was deep anger inside everyone's heart as death was directly attributed to the injuries inflicted. Lord Irwin, the Viceroy and Sir John Simon, too, offered their condolences but these were not sufficient to compensate the loss of self-pride.

The funeral was attended by nearly one and half lakh persons. All citizens, independent of their religious beliefs, observed mourning. Though Lalaji, of late, had distanced himself from revolutionaries as well as Congress and was recognized as being communal, there was no doubt in any mind about his stature as a leader of national fame. Therefore, the assault over him was regarded as a big challenge to the vigour of the nation.

Sensing the mood of the public, Bhagat Singh proposed before the group about avenging the death of Lalaji. He also suggested that ten British must be killed for loss of one Indian life.

The Lahore body accepted to forward this resolution before Hindustan Socialist Republican Army. A message regarding meeting was immediately forwarded to Chandra Shekhar Azad, Commander-in-Chief who was underground after the Kakori case. Rajguru, who was ill at the time of Lalaji's death, also started from Pune. via Kashi and Firozepur for Lahore. A new chapter in Indian history was about to be written.

Organizing the act

The year 17th November, 1928 was one of darkest days in the history of India as one of her great sons was brutally killed. The revolutionaries had decided to avenge the loss and started making efforts in this direction. This very day, Chandra Shekhar Azad, Rajguru, Mahaveer Singh and many other revolutionaries arrived in Lahore.

Jai Gopal was eagerly waiting for his leader at Lahore Cantonment Railway Station at 7 a.m., while Sukhdev very patiently waited outside. Azad, carrying a black suitcase, alighted from a passenger train, accompanied by Mahaveer Singh (Code name Pratap Singh). Handing him the suitcase, Azad directed Jai Gopal to wait for next express train to gather two more members and then escort them to the Mozang House. Azad went out of station to meet Sukhdev, who was waiting for him and Mahaveer Singh continued his journey by that train to Lahore Railway Station.

After a little while, Rajguru alias 'M', along with Kundan Lal, too arrived by the express train. He had come here to play a most significant role in one of the most important operations in the history of revolutionary movement. Jai Gopal took them, and the suitcase given by Azad to Mozang House, which was taken on rent by Mahaveer Singh to serve as the headquarters for all operations. Mahaveer Singh had already reached there through some other route. Meeting old friends gave immense pleasure to Rajguru.

Thereafter Jai Gopal proceeded to meet Sukhdev and Azad, who were relaxing in the room of Desraj, in the boarding house of D.A.V. College. Azad immediately enquired about safety of the suitcase and asked Jai Gopal to fetch it, to which, he promptly complied.

Azad opened the suitcase and to Jai Gopal's utter astonishment, it contained a mini armamentairium. The weapons included a Mouser pistol, a revolver (which was Exhibit P 200 in Lahore Conspiracy case), a small revolver, (which was recovered from Sukhdev by Police on search), another revolver (with which, Rajguru had killed Saunders) a knife (which was Exhibit P. 476 in Lahore Conspiracy case), and ten to twelve cartridges. Azad explained the method of loading and unloading the revolver to his colleagues and then, carefully placed them back in the suitcase. Jai Gopal took the suitcase back to Mozang House at around 9.p.m.

Azad, Bhagat Singh, Rajguru, Mahaveer Singh and Kishori Lal spent the night at Mozang House, discussing the future plans. The discussions ultimately resulted in the unsuccessful robbery attempt but they were successful in the killing of Saunders. They continued to occupy this place till about four days of killing Saunders. The building was a rented facility and was located near *Kabristan* (grave yard), away from population to escape the detection by Police. This was the headquarters for all the revolutionaries, frequently visited by local accomplices like Jai Gopal, Hans Raj Vohra and Kalicharan. Later, before the Lahore Conspircy Case Tribunal, neighbouring residents Hussain Bakhsh (PW 64), Buddhu (PW 73) and Gaman (PW 74) had testified for prosecution regarding the frequent visits by Jai Gopal and Hansraj Vohra to the Mozang House.

The team was desperate to avenge the death of Lalaji but felt frustrated because of paucity of funds. To tackle this problem, the group, in late November 1928, decided to attempt robbery on Punjab National Bank, Lahore in early December 1928.

On 3rd December night, Azad delegated the task to Bhagat Singh, Sukhdev, Rajguru, Mahaveer Singh, Kishori Lal, Jai Gopal, Hans Raj Vohra and Kalicharan. The plan was to be executed the next day, 4th December, 1928. Bhagat Singh was asked to arrange a taxi for quick escape at exactly 3 p.m. on that day. Kalicharan was handed over the knife to cut the telephone line, to sever the communication link. Sukhdev was handed the revolver, to be used to restrain the guard at entry gate of the bank, snatch his gun and arrange the currency notes in two bags after looting. Finally, Azad, along with his team mates, was to drive the taxi himself to a safe place.

Azad, along with Bhagat Singh and Mahaveer Singh, had visited the Bank several times and had observed all details. He and Mahaveer Singh had several trial runs with the taxi between Lahore Gate and Mureedke. The weapons were already with them.

Everybody was alert, as planned, at his specified position on 4th December afternoon for the designated role. Azad and Sukhdev armed themselves with the mouser and a gun. Kalicharan was provided with the knife and gun. Bhagat Singh and Mahaveer Singh, both armed with a gun, left to get the taxi while rest of the team gathered and started waiting patiently for them in front of the Bank. The clock struck three, but both of them had still not turned up. Everybody truned suspicious and apprehensive.

A little later, Mahaveer Singh appeared, alighting from a *tonga* (horse driven cart). He whispered a few words in the ears of Azad and to everybody's surprise Azad signalled them to march back.

After returning to Mozang House, Azad informed Rajguru that failure to drive the taxi was the root cause of aborting this operation. Later, before the Lahore Conspiracy Case Tribunal, Jai Gopal blamed the non-availability of the vehicle as the prime reason while, Choudhary Roshanlal, Magistrate First Class, Lahore (PW 29), referring to confession by Mahaveer Singh, stated Azad's failed attempt. Sukhdev's remarks in the proceeding book also supported the later version.

Barkat Ali, the taxi driver (PW 87) had deposed before the Tribunal on 15th July, 1929 that about one and three quarters of a year back, two persons had hired his taxi at Railway Station for Shalimar Garden and spent around one and a half hour in the vehicle. One of them attempted to drive the carriage but was unsuccessful. Then, the other person got down, hired the tonga driven by Firoz and left, while the other person continued his journey till Shalimar Garden. He identified Bhagat Singh and Mahaveer Singh as those two passengers. Admitting that a taxi driver has to entertain so many clients in a day, it appears quite unnatural that Barkat Ali could have remembered their faces after such a long passage of time. Therefore, Sukhdev, in his remarks in the proceeding book, regarded Barkat Ali as tutored witness and refused to believe the taxi driver, whose conveyance was hired on 4th December.

Jai Gopal (PW 2) and Hansraj Vohra, both approvers, had stated before the Tribunal that on reaching Punjab

National Bank, they had sighted Rajguru standing with other colleagues. The tribunal inferred Rajguru's participation in Punjab National Bank robbery case on the basis of these statements. In reality, Rajguru never took part in this operation. During the planning phase, Rajguru had enquired from Azad about his role in this operation. To this Azad had clearly replied that he was not included in this mission but was chosen to play the leading role in next event (Saunders' murder).

The Tribunal, in the judgment, clearly mentioned that Rajguru had specifically been called at Lahore to serve the vital role of a sharp shooter in both, Punjab National Bank Robbery as well as Saunders' murder cases. This mention about his involvement in the robbery conspiracy is absolutely unreal and false.

The financial crisis had left the group to subsist in scarcity and pitiable circumstances, a situation not new to Rajguru. The failed attempt, however, could not deter the revolutionaries from their path and they soon started to plan their next mission, the killing of Scott.

In the meantime, Bhagat Singh, Rajguru, Bhagwan Das and Vijay Kumar Sinha went to attend a public meeting in Bradlaugh Hall, arranged to pay tributes to Kakori Case martyrs, in which their portraits were being exhibited with the help of a magic lantern. To the dismay of viewers, the pictures were not clear due to distorted focus on the curtain. Bhagat Singh asked Rajguru and Bhagwan Das to go on the stage and shift the projector a little forwards as he could not do it himself because of the risk of being identified by the public. Rajguru, too, was not willing to go to stage and he kept shouting to others. Finally, Bhagat Singh left Rajguru there and took Sinha and Bhagwandas with him and they all went to see the movie 'Uncle Tom's Cabin.'

The revenge

The group, with fresh zeal, decided to implement their next plan, avenging the death of Lalaji. The group had indeed planned to assassinate, J.C. Scott, Senior Superintendent of Police, Lahore, who had ordered the lathi charge and was, thus, held by the revolutionaries as being the chief perpetrator. But destiny chose Saunders, the person who had actually delivered the fatal blow, to pay the price, instead.

A meeting, under the chairmanship of Azad, the Commander-in-Chief was organized at Mozang House on the night of 10th December, 1928. Four out of seven Central Committee members attended the meeting. Bhagat Singh, seconded by others, put forward the resolution that action must be taken to avenge the death of Lalaji, which will also send a strong message to the World that India was not going to tolerate this barbarous act of injustice.

They finally decided to avenge the insult to the nation by killing Scott. Everybody volunteered but Sukhdev was chosen by the group as the coordinator for this mission. Sukhdev, in turn, named Azad, Bhagat Singh, Rajguru and Jai Gopal as his accomplices to accomplish the task.

Rajguru felt exhilarated as his life long wish to serve his motherland was being fulfilled. He was chosen for his shooting skills and now, was liked by all members for his bravery and jovial nature. He had rather started announcing before his friends that one day, he and only he would shoot Scott.

Jai Gopal was assigned the duty of watching the route and record office timings and movements of Scott and fellow officers with precision. He, later, turned approver and deposed before the Tribunal on 7th May 1930, "I kept watch on Scott at Police Headquarters from 11th to 14th December 1928 and regularly informed Panditji (Azad) that Scott comes to office usually between ten to eleven a.m. and goes back at four to five p.m. Panditji had planned the killing on 15th December as Kakori Day was scheduled to be celebrated on 16th. On 15th, neither Scott nor his car no. 6728 was sighted. This was communicated to Panditji in the afternoon only.

The plan was changed according to suggestions by Jai Gopal in the meeting, held on 15th night. Azad also provided the tips on safe escape to Bhagat Singh and Rajguru. On 16th all the members visited Bradlaugh Hall to pay homage to Kakori case martyrs.

17th December 1928

Jai Gopal, as usual, was on alert watch outside the Police Headquarters since 09.30 in the morning. At around ten, he saw an European Police Officer climbing down from the motorcycle. Jai Gopal had never seen Scott himself so he took the European for Scott, in reality, he was Saunders, Assistant SP, clad in almost identical uniform. Scott had not come as he was on leave that day. Jai Gopal informed Azad about this.

Azad discussed the prospects with Sukhdev, Bhagat Singh, Rajguru and Jai Gopal between 1.30 to two p.m. and decided to expedite the killing that afternoon itself. Azad kept the Mouser and gave revolver to Rajguru and Brownie automatic pistol to Bhagat Singh. Rajguru went by foot while Azad, Bhagat Singh and Jai Gopal rode on the bicycles. Two bicycles were put near D.A.V. College.

At around 4 p.m., Jai Gopal stood with a bicycle on the road in front of Police Headquarters, pretending to make some repairs. Rajguru and Bhagat Singh were standing slightly away from the main gate.

Jai Gopal saw an European Police Officer, wearing a felt cap, start a red coloured motorcycle. The confusion was still persisting. He took Saunders for Scott again and made the fateful signal to Rajguru. Saunders started moving slowly towards the main gate. As he (Saunders) neared, Rajguru at once fired.

The shot was accurate. The bullet pierced the chest and Saunders collapsed on the ground, with one leg under the running motorcycle. Bhagat Singh immediately realized that they had picked the wrong man but had no option. He fired several shots at Saunders to make sure that he was dead.

Bhagat Singh and Rajguru then ran into Court Street towards D.A.V. College, while Jai Gopal kept standing at the turning. Traffic inspector W.J. Feam, accompanied by Head Constable Chanan Singh and one more constable, on witnessing the killing, started chasing them, Rajguru tried to fire at him but missed. The second attempt resulted in a misfire but Rajguru, somehow, managed to retrieve the empty cartridge. Feam fell down into a drain and hurt his arm. Feam and the constable stopped but Chanan Singh continued the chase.

Both ran into D.A.V. College compound through the gate near Principal's residence. Azad was already there. Despite warning by Azad and Feam, Chanan Singh dared to enter the premises. Azad fired a shot, hitting Chanan Singh on thighs. Second shot resulted in his collapse. He finally died one hour later at Maya Hospital, Lahore. Then no one dared to pursue them.

Bhagat Singh, Rajguru and Azad then crossed the dividing wall and entered the hostel. They stayed at the roof for a while, making sure that no one was chasing them. Then they rode off to Dev Samaj Road, crossed Gole Bag and proceeded towards Secretariat. The trio eventually reached Mozang House safely.

The Police reached after some time. The area was cordoned off. Frantic searches were made in all hostel rooms and all residents were subjected to intense interrogation but there was no clue. The shooters seemed to have dissolved into thin air.

The thrill gripped the whole City. The residents had mixed feelings of pride as well as apprehension.

It was an irony that on that fateful evening the heroes, who managed to destablize the Government, did not have enough money to get food. Jai Gopal borrowed ten rupees from his friend, Banshilal and made the arrangements.

The revolutionaries had aimed to kill Scott but ended up killing Saunders, the person who actually had delivered the fatal blow. Saunders, 25 to 26 years old, probationary Indian Police Services Officer had been instrumental in disbanding an anti-Government group, only a year ago. He was the son-in-law of P.A. to the Governor of Punjab and already had contributed an article in the departmental journal, 'Blackhood'.

Bhagwandas praised the shooting skills of Rajguru. Rajguru was not enthusiastic and said, "Leave it. I had aimed for his skull but the bullet hit him on the chest." Bhagwandas checked the weapon and remaining cartridges and noted that cartridges actually fitted within the bore loosely and this difference was actually responsible for missed aim.

All the roads had been sealed. The station was under intense surveillance by Police and C.I.D. including some of the eye witnesses. The police was apprehending all suspects, making vigorous raids and searches. It was not safe for them to continue staying at Lahore and all members had been asked to take maximum precautions to conceal their identify and find the safe way out at the earliest.

Next day morning brought another new sensation. Several pink posters, many of them hand written, were found affixed at various public places in Lahore. They bore the heading. "Saunders is dead, Lalaji is avenged" and were signed by Balraj, Commander-in-Chief, HSRA. This infused the joy among the public and despair in the administration. The entire text was as follows:

Notice

By Hindustan Socialist Republican Army

'Bureaucracy Beware'

With the death of J.P. Saunders, the assassination of Lala Lajpat Rai has been avenged.

It is a matter of great regret that a respected leader of 30 crores of people was attacked by an ordinary police officer like J.P. Saunders and met with his death at his mean hands. This national insult was a challenge to young men.

Today the World has seen that the people of India are not lifeless; their blood has not become cold. They can lay down their lives for the country's honour. The proof of this has been given by the youth who are ridiculed and insulted by the leaders of their own country.

Tyrant Government Beware

Do not hurt the feelings of the oppressed suffering people of this country. Stop your devilish ways. Despite all your laws preventing us from keeping arms and despite your watchfulness, people of this country would continue to get pistols and revolvers. Even if these arms are not adequate in numbers for an armed revolution. they would be sufficient for avenging the insult to the country's honour. Even if our own people condemn us and ridicule us and if the foreign government subjects us to any amount of repression, we shall all be ever ready to teach a lesson to foreign tyrants who insult our national honour. Despite all opposition and repression, we shall carry forward the call for revolution and even if we go to the scaffold for being hanged, we shall continue to shout:

LONG LIVE REVOLUTION!

We are sorry to have killed a man. But this man was a part of cruel, despicable and unjust system and killing him was a necessity. This man has been killed as an employee of the British Government. This Government is the most oppressive government in the world.

We are sorry for shedding human blood but it becomes necessary to bathe the altar of revolution with blood. Our aim is to bring about a revolution which would end all exploitation of man by man.

LONG LIVE REVOLUTION!

18th December 1928

sd/-
Balraj
Commander-in-Chief,
H.S.R.A.

Finding the safe passage was one of the most difficult tasks and for this, Sukhdev had an innovative idea. He contacted Durga *Bhabhi*, wife of fellow revolutionary Bhagwati Charan, on 19th December 1928 at around 5 a.m. at Shiv Niwas (name of her residence). Bhagwati Charan had gone to Calcutta to attend the convention of All India Congress Committee.

Sukhdev hesitatingly asked, "Can you leave Lahore with somebody as his wife. Shachi (her three years old son) would also accompany. We need to help one of the Saunders' killers."

On receiving an affirmative reply, Sukhdev further warned that the task involved great danger as there might be firing and bloodshed anytime. *Durga Bhabhi* promptly handed over five hundred rupees to Sukhdev for making arrangements. Less than 24 hours had been left for grand escape.

Azad, Bhagat Singh and Rajguru had already left Mozang House at 5 a.m. Bhagat Singh, wearing an overcoat and hat, along with his servant Rajguru, reached Shiv Niwas at about 11 a.m. Sukhdev asked *Bhabhi* whether she could recognize the young man. Seeing Durga *Bhabhi's* confusion. Bhagat Singh joyfully said, "Now I can relax as there is least chance of recognition by the Police." *Bhabhi* then exclaimed "Bhagat Singh!" Then, there was laughter all around.

Rajguru was donning the garb of a servant. With dark complexion and tonsured head, wearing dirty rags, and holding a box and a torn sheet in hands, he did not require any make up. He occupied a cot near the toilet. Despite Bhagat Singh's insistence, he refused to come in even for meals, like an ardent servant. Durga Devi never pardoned herself for this treatment given to Rajguru though she was not responsible for it.

Sukhdev left and both spent the night at Shiv Niwas.

On 20th December, all here reached Lahore Railway Station at 5 a.m. Bhagat Singh donned the attire of an officer with obliquely placed felt cap, overcoat with raised collars, his left hand holding the three years old Shachi and right hand tucked inside his pocket, fondling the gun. Durga Devi, clad in modern clothes and high heeled sandals, looked a perfect officer's wife. Rajguru, wearing a pyjama and coat, a turban over his head and a neatly folded dupatta around his waist, walked behind the duo holding a box folded in old rag.

The station looked chaotic as security forces were searching the assassins like wild dogs. They purchased

Rajguru's house in Khed

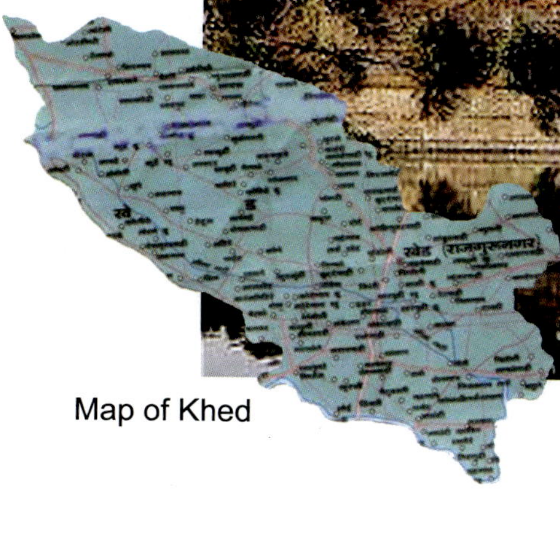

Map of Khed

Rajguru Nagar

Birthplace of Rajguru

जन्मरास :- कर्क जन्मनक्षत्र :- पुष्य २ रे चरण

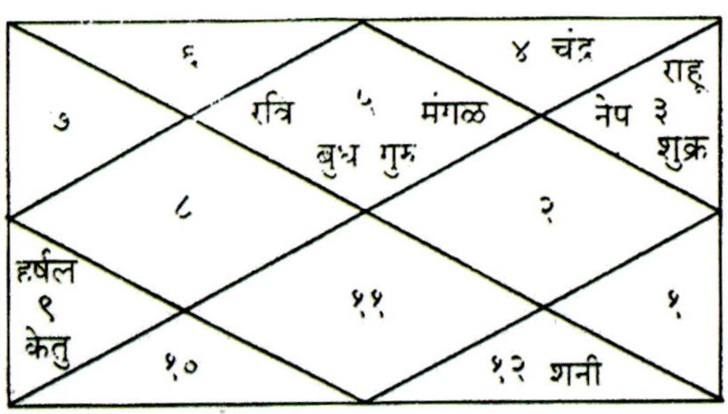

जन्मदिनांक :- २४ ऑगस्ट १९०८. मिती : श्रावण व. १३ शके १८२९

जन्म वेळ :- सूर्योदयापूर्वी, जन्म लग्न :- सिंह

जन्म वार :- सोमवार शनि वक्री, गुरु वक्री

Horoscope of Rajguru

Parvati Bai (Rajguru's mother)

Shivram Hari Rajguru

Rajguru's mother Parvati Bai with the family of Bhagat Singh

Rajguru's Nephew with his sons

two first class and one third class tickets for 14 Down Dehradun Express. The couple occupied the first class seat, moving in an unhurried manner, without arousing any suspicion. Rajguru, too, walked patiently to his compartment.

Leisure time

Rajguru left Bhagat Singh and Durga *Bhabhi* at Lucknow and reached Kashi via Kanpur and Agra. He then disclosed the whole Lahore affair to Savargaonkar, including his own role. Savargaonkar had already learnt of the events from Azad.

Rajguru resumed his gymnasium, imparting training to about 35 youth. It was located in front of a police station near *Nagri Pracharni Sabha*. But this did not induce any fear in Rajguru's mind.

The activities were put on a standstill for three to four months because of intensified police surveillance after Saunders' murder. Then revolutionaries started shifting the centre of activities to Agra because of two reasons. Firstly, the planning for seeking forced release of Yogesh Chandra Chatterjee, a Kakori Case convict was underway and secondly, in Agra was located one of the three bomb factories Bhagat Singh had established in collaboration with West Bengal colleagues.

The revolutionaries rented two houses, one at *Heeng ki Mandi* and another at *Nai ki Mandi*. In *Heeng ki Mandi* house, Yatindra Nath Das and H.K. Mukherjee imparted training to various colleagues in handling bombs. Bhagat Singh, Azad, Sukhdev, Fanindra Nath Ghosh, Bijoy Kumar Sinha and many others stayed with them for months. His sleeping habits and jovial nature, at times, were instrumental in creating many humorous situations.

Jaidev Kapoor and Bhagwandas Mahore were included in the planning for seeking forced release of Yogesh Chandra Chatterjee. Sadashiv Malkapurkar was asked to fetch Bhangwandas from Gwalior while Rajguru had to visit Saharanpur to fetch Jaidev Kapoor. Sinha detailed everything to Rajguru and handed him over some cash. He also instructed him to hand over this cash to Kapoor and ask him not to spend at all or sparingly, if needed and return the remaining amount to Agra as this was acutely needed here. The half asleep Rajguru replied in affirmative. He and Sadashiv left for their destination from *Raja ki Mandi* railway station.

Next day Sadashiv returned with Bhagwandas but Rajguru had not yet come back. He turned up one day later, but all alone. Sinha presumed that Kapoor (Code name Harish) was playing a prank and was in the hiding. He crossed the main gate and looked in the street too, but Kapoor was not in sight. Now he asked Rajguru . "Where is Harish? Where you have sent him ? He was to be brought here only."

Rajguru was dumb-founded as not only he had not brought Kapoor with him but also had handed over the whole amount to Kapoor and asked him to spend the money as he liked and contain himself within the house. Kapoor told him that he was expecting a call from Agra. Rajguru, even then, continued to give him the same instructions. Actually, in half sleep, Rajguru had hardly listened to Sinha's words and interpreted that as Kapoor's residence was hardly known, to one or two persons hence, would be kept safe in house after his release.

Now it was Sinha's turn to beat his head as they had been deprived of one useful hand as well as invaluable money at this hour of need. He expressed his great displeasure over this foolishness. When he communicated this to Azad, he received a reprimand instead. "What was the need of sending a spoilsport like him?" But when Sinha told him about Rajguru's opinion about using Saharanpur as a safe house, Azad turned appreciative and whole tension vanished.

One day, Rajguru could not be traced in either of the houses at Agra. A search for him in nearby places also yielded no result. There was great anxiety as none of them used to leave the premises without informing. Everybody wondered over his whereabouts and safety. After all efforts, when he was not found, Azad, following the guide lines of the HSRA, ordered the vacation of house as he thought it highly probable that Rajguru was apprehended by the police.

The compliance started at a rapid pace, Sadashiv had hung his long loin cloth on two nails in the wall to dry. As he pulled the cloth, he to his greatest astonishment, saw Rajguru sleeping, standing along the wall. He immediately called Azad and other colleagues to witness the grand scenario. Greatly amused, they started singing in a chorus:

Bhaye Pragat Kripala. Gadbadjhala, Kumbharkarna Awatari! (Here appers to bless us, the ever confusing reincarnation of Kumbhkarna)

The noise disturbed Rajguru from sleep. He said, "I had somehow managed the solitude but here too, you are disturbing me."

Sinha teased him, "Rajguru deserves a special prize for finding out his innovative way of sleeping." Rajguru maintained that he should be allowed to sleep as a way of prize.

Bhagwandas let another one loose, "You can compete with *Kumbhakarna*. Rather his tale appears to be a myth." Rajguru was not to give up and said. "No, it is not so. Rather, by seeing my sleep, you should now start believing on that historical reality."

His sleepy habits and friendly duets with Bhagat Singh were a constant source of laughter among the colleagues. Both were travelling back from Mathura to Agra. They arrived at the station at eleven in the night, much earlier than scheduled 2 a.m. departure. Bhagat Singh found it hard to resist his sleep as he had been awake for the past two nights. He, though, did not trust Rajguru but still took a chance. He asked, "Please listen to what I say. I find it difficult to keep awake at the moment. If you take responsibility then I can have an hour's sleep."

Rajguru obligingly replied. "Why not, why do you consider me so irresponsible? You lie down and I will wake you up at the correct hour."

Bhagat Singh handed over his overcoat, cautioned him, in whispering tone, about the gun inside the pocket and asked to be woken up at 1.30. Rajguru occupied the seat and Bhagat Singh went into deep sleep instantly. His sleep was distrubed at around four a.m. by noise in the waiting room. He arose abruptly just to find Rajguru devouring sleep on another bench.

In frustration, he kicked the bench. Now Rajguru arose, rubbing his eye, and said. "What happened? I swear by you I do not know as to what has happened."

Rajguru though not having good looks, was a devout worshipper of beauty. One day, he brought a calendar having a preety picture of a bathing woman and hung it on the wall. Azad came in the room after he had left. A smiling Vaishampayan drew his attention towards the calender. In irritation, Azad just pulled away the calendar, tore it in pieces and threw it in the garbage can.

Rajguru , upon his return, found the calendar missing and made a loud enquiry about it. Smilingly, Vaishampayan pointed towards the garbage heap.

Rajguru, in great anger, thundered, "Who did it?"

Azad was equally loud, "me."

Rajguru was little subdued. Picking up a few torn pieces, he asked in a lower tone, "Why did you? I liked it so much."

Azad was angry. "how are we concerned with such pictures?"

Rajguru, still feeling the loss, continued. "It was so beautiful."

Azad was still boiling. "how are we concerned with beauty?"

Now Rajguru was also fuming. "So would you demolish what is beautiful?"

Azad said, "Yes."

Rajguru threw a challenge. "Then, go and demolish Taj Mahal."

Azad was now trembling in anger, "Yes, I will, if I can."

Now Rajguru was suddenly quiet. After a minute, in a slow tone, he said. "We want to make the world beautiful. This can not be accomplished by breaking and demolising the beautiful things."

These unexpected words of wisdom from Rajguru greatly softened Azad. He now explained, in affectionate tone, to Rajguru, "I did not mean it. We have left our families to lead this life for a singular goal of seeking independence. I desire that we all, remain focused on it so that we can achieve it. I am afraid that your love for beauty may become a distraction from our path or a troublesome weakness for you." These soothing words calmed Rajguru too and he was his usual self again.

Once, the group visited Taj Mahal, the great architectural marvel and a symbol of love. The sight of incomparable beauty of the monument in the moonlit night made them all spellbound. Sinha, by singing a Bengali song, surcharged the atmosphere.

Everybody, quietly engrossed were staring at the Taj. Rajguru, not overwhelmed by emotions, wanted to chat and thus was a disturbance to silent meditation of his colleagues. Everybody was, thus, avoiding him. One of them even remarked sarcastically, "Why have you come here? Better go home and do wrestling."

A helpless Rajguru also occupied a silent place and started contemplating. He created a *Sher* (couplet) out of his thought but none took heed of him.

He had his opportunity to express his thought next day when all colleagues, over a cup of tea, were discussing the moon light beauty of Taj. Observing them in a lighter mood. Rajguru presented them with his creation:

Ab tak nahin maloom tha ishq kya cheez hai,
Roje ko dekh kar mere bhi ishq ne balwa kiya

(I did not know till now as to what love is. My love too revolted by witnessing *Roja* (fast).

Everybody had a hilarious laugh at the words *Ishq ne balwa kiya*. Sinha was jumping uncontrollably while Batukeshwar Dutt just kept staring at the great poet. Bhagat Singh took out the gun from his pocket, handed it over to Rajguru, pointing towards his chest and said "Rajguru, press the trigger to put the bullet in my chest. Shoot all of us rather than your *Sher* otherwise promise us that you will never write any *sher* (lion) or any funny gimmick like this."

Rajguru had the knack of making others laugh, even by ridiculing himself. Once, he presented a line from a *ghazal* (Urdu poetry):

Hum to mashik hai ji aashook ki fankari ke

This again caused everybody to laugh aloud. Rajguru could not understand the reason. Then, Bhagwandas had to explain that you had distorted the words by jumbling *Aashook* for *Mashook* and *Mashik* for *Aashik*. This had Rajguru smile too.

Once, Azad refused to listen to Rajguru's creations. Rajguru asked him to sing a song instead. Azad asked him to keep a watch on the road. Rajguru asked whether he was apprehensive of arrival of police.

Azad replied, "I am not apprehensive of arrival of police, but of washer man or porter. Any of them could come searching for his donkey." Then he, in heavy voice, started singing seriously:

Maa, Hume Vidaa do, Jaate hain hum Vijayketu Fehrane Ko

(Mother, bid me farewell. I proceed to hoist the victory flag).

Rajguru interrupted. "There he comes."

Azad enquired, "Who? Washer man or the porter."

Rajguru replied, "None of them, but the police man."

A meeting was going on in *Hing ki Mandi* house at Agra in 1929. Azad detailed all the colleagues about the torture techniques adopted by the police to extract the desired information from the arrested suspects and their impact on the body and mind of the victim. He maintained that it would be better if one is not apprehended otherwise in event of impending capture by police, when no other option is left, it would be better to fight and die.

Rajguru, being on mess duty that day, was cooking food in the kitchen. His attention was totally focused on Azad's words and was deeply influenced by them. He wondered as to how he would fare in such circumstances. To test his tolerance, he immediately picked up a tong and placed it in the fire of the burner. When it had turned red hot, he picked it and touched it over his chest. There was immediate severe pain and burning of the skin. Without flinching, he repeated the act seven times despite severe agony.

During the night, while asleep, Rajguru moaned in pain. Azad was sleeping near him. The sound disturbed his sleep and he enquired about the cause of the discomfort. At first, Rajguru tried to avoid the question but was forced to state the fact on Azad's insistence.

Azad asked Rajguru to take his shirt off. Rajguru silently complied. Azad was shocked to observe five big blisters over the chest under the candle light. Azad was so much moved that his eye became immediately wet with tears out of deep affection and faith in Rajguru.

Going to a doctor for treatment was far to dangerous and so out of question; hence only home remedy was provided. However, this episode served to prove to all colleagues that this person definitely belonged to a different class.

Just before his hanging, Susheela Didi happened to visit him in Central Jail, Lahore. Remembering this episode, she with great respect, requested Rajguru. "Brother, I request you to fulfull the desire of this poor sister of seeing the scars over your chest."

Rajguru was wearing the attire of a death convict. This included cotton underwear, a cotton half sleeved shirt and a circular cap. He was destined to put such clothes on, whether as a drill master or as a convict. His iron face, however, started glowing at these words. With a smile, he loosened the buttons and exposed his chest.

Susheela Didi had witnessed the five glowing symbols of determination of a true patriot.

दृढ़ता की गाथा का ब्यान कर रहे थे।

More glimpses

Rajguru, though by appearance quite rigid, possessed a tender heart too. He was always eager to encounter death without fear. He never lost his humour, even in the face of imminent death.

Rajguru was very talkative and it was very hard to stop him once he started chatting. Once, he was travelling by train with Azad and Bhagwandas, disguised as illiterate labourer from Kanpur to Jhansi. Azad spotted some secret police personnel also travelling in the same compartment. He asked Bhagwandas to sing some cheap poetry and himself started to praise the recital in a language, used by loafers.

After sometime, the train arrived at Kalpi on Bundelkhand border. The sight of uneven landscape reminded Rajguru of guerilla warfare tactics used by the great warrior, Shivajee. He suddenly forgot that he was evading the police disguised as an illiterate labourer. Pointing towards the cave like openings on the hillock, he started saying. "Panditji, is it not a good place for guerilla warfare?" Azad, exercising restraint, pretending not to hear Rajguru, asked Bhagwandas to repeat the lines he was narrating.

Rajguru, still not understanding, repeated, "it bears great resemblance to the location chosen by Shivajee." Azad, now on the verge of losing patience, continued to praise Bhagwandas without paying heed to a surprised Rajguru. Later Rajguru understood his mistake and stopped chatting.

After they had reached the destination. Azad started shouting at Bhagwandas, "You people always blame me for shouting at Ragunath (Code name for Rajguru). Look at him. He foolishly talks about Shivajee and guerilla warfare in front of secret police, which were on our trail." Then he embraced Rajguru and said, "But I appreciate your observation, the place is fit for such warfare and we will use it as and when needed."

Once, Rajguru and Bhagat Singh were required to go from Agra to Delhi by night train. Their master-servant disguise had helped them escape and saved them from being apprehended after Saunders' murder. They decided to repeat the time-tested tactics.

When they left the house at night, Bhagat Singh picked up the larger trunk as he thought that later Rajguru, as servant, would have to carry it so he should help him at this time in the dark. Rajguru took the attache case and bag with him. On Bhagat Singh's instruction, Rajguru fetched a tonga.

Rajguru came back, sitting on the back seat of the tonga, He forgot that he was playing the role of a servant and called Bhagat Singh to sit near him like a friend. Rajguru somehow managed to put luggage on the tonga with the help of cart driver. Bhagat Singh signalled Rajguru to occupy the front seat, as it was used routinely by the menials.

They reached the railway station. Bhagat Singh bought a second class ticket for himself and a third class ticket for Rajguru. Now he took the attache case, leaving the other two articles for Rajguru.

Waiting for train, Bhagat Singh started to stroll. Rajguru, with large trunk and bag in his hands, started to walk by the side of him. To shake him off, Bhagat Singh quickened the pace but Rajguru was not to give up. Bhagat Singh, now, decided to stop. Rajguru too stopped and said. "Tired? I am not tired despite carrying this much luggage."

Bhagat Singh, in frustration, pointed towards a seat without looking at him and scolded. "Look here, servant, you sit there." This brought Rajguru back to his senses.

Money was a vital necessity for the functioning of the organization. Though Azad did not prefer robbery after the Kakori case but he was forced to accept the resolution of robbing a math (shrine) to resolve the ever soaring financial crisis.

It was decided that a hermit, living on the banks of holy river, Ganges, at Kanpur, supposedly in possession of valuable jewels, should be robbed. The booty should be sold in Rajasthan and the amount, thus collected, should be used to procure the weapons.

Azad chose Shiv Verma, Rajguru and Bhagwandas for this mission. Shiv Verma, being the organizer for Central provinces, arranged four more local accomplices through Pooranchand Sanak.

They reached the shrine in the evening. The *ghat* was deserted but the shrine was filled with followers. Azad and Rajguru entered the premises, directing others to wait outside. Both bowed before the hermit and sat on one side. The place was filled with smoke of tobaaco and marijuana. Though both were absolute non-smokers, just to follow the tradition and not to appear too obvious, they also devoured few puffs from the *chilam*, unhesitatingly.

Azad had already taken stock of the situation. After twenty minutes, both walked out and Azad signalled his companions to walk back, saying that there was to be no action. Upon enquiry, he replied that, "The success in this mission can only be achieved after killing a number of innocent persons. It is not proper to sacrifice precious human lives for such a trivial cause, when we are not even sure that our desired object is actually in his possession."

On the way as they were returning in a dejected mood, they saw a person putting some *pooja utara* or *totka* (left over after worshipping deliberately left to be consumed by cattle) on a crossing. Azad asked Bhagwandas (Code name - Kailash) to collect the cash, sweets, coconut and other offerings from it, so that they could draw some consolation by not returning empty handed.

Bhagwandas went there but could not find any such articles, in frustration, he kicked the burning *diya* (earthen lamp).

On returning, Azad asked, "Yes, what did you bring."

Bhagwandas replied, "Nothing. There was only one *diya* with little ghee inside."

Azad said, "I knew, you will never act wise. After putting out *diya*, you should have consumed the ghee at least. Whose face had you seen in the morning?"

Bhagwandas sheepishly replied, "Yours."

Azad now smiled, "You are lying as after seeing my face, you were bound to do something. It is said:

Prat lei jo naam hamara; ta din tahi naa mile aahara!"

(Whoever remembers me in the morning, he is destined to spend that day without food)

One of the chief objectives of shifting headquarters to Agra was to have Yogeshchandra Chatterjee, a Kakori case convict, released by force. The plan had been aborted once as authorities decided to delay his shifting to some other jail for a few months. When they received the information of his proposed shifting this time, they decided to get him released in the train during the transit.

Batukeshwar Dutt was entrusted with the job of watching the Railway Station. On 16th February, 1929, he informed that Chatterjee was to be shifted by 7 p.m. train. He would be kept at Kanpur during the night and then taken to Lucknow by next morning train. The revolutionaries aimed at attempting his release in train between Kanpur and Lucknow.

Rajguru, on Azad's directives, travelled in the same train to Kanpur. He was to arrange for a safe house in Kanpur. Azad, along with Bhagat Singh, Bhagwandas Mahore, Vijay Kumar Sinha, Sadashiv and Shiv Verma, boarded the train to Kanpur at 10 p.m.

It was not acceptable to the cruel destiny. Rajguru failed to arrange a safe house overnight. To make the matters worse, Azad's pocket was picked at Kanpur Railway Station, resulting in loss of valuable cash and driving license. Azad had no option but to order his colleagues to return. They witnessed the sight of a dejected Chatterjee, walking cordoned by police men, with a heavy heart, Rajguru too returned with Sadashiv to Agra on 18th February.

At Agra, one fine evening Azad was sitting with Rajguru, Bhagat Singh, Sukhdev, Batukeshwar Dutt, Shiv Verma and other colleagues. They started, in a lighter vein, discussing what fate each one was likely to meet.

Regarding Dutt (Code name Mohan), everyone opined that he would be apprehended in a park on a moonlit night, gazing uniterruptedly at the moon and speaking to the police men, "No problem with the arrest, but look how beautiful the moon is."

Bhagat Singh (Code name Ranjeet) and Bijoy Kumar Sinha (Code name Bachchu) were most expected to be caught at a theatre, watching a movie and on apprehension, to request police men, "It is all right. We will come with you, but, only after the movie is over."

Azad was expected to be apprehended in an unconscious state, following some treacherous act of a traitor, while hunting in the woods of Bundelkhand. He would then be shifted to Jhansi hospital and subsequently hanged.

Azad smiled at this funny idea. Bhagat Singh tickled further, "For you, two ropes will be needed, one around your neck and another around your abdomen." Azad, smilingly, caressed the Mouser and said, "Hanging is reserved for people like you. No one can dare to touch me during my life as long as I have this gun with me."

Regarding Rajguru, everybody unanimously resolved that he would sure be caught while sleeping as he is capable of sleeping even in a standing posture. When his eyes would open in police lock up, he would ask the guard whether this is a dream or reality.

The visionary Azad had indeed forecasted the future for himself, Bhagat Singh and Rajguru. As transpired later, Azad died while firing till last moment, Bhagat Singh was hanged and Rajguru was apprehended, while sleeping. Did the destiny reveal itself on that day from the mouth of these great warriors?

The revolutionaries had great success in bomb making and testing at Agra. They also opened bomb factories at some other places. These successes, coupled with failed mission of Chatterjee's release, had served to take a huge burden off their shoulders and reduced the need of staying at the headquarters for them. Everybody was, thus given the freedom to move about.

There is no authentic information on Rajguru's whereabouts between this period and assault on Viceroy in March 1929. According to the Marathi book, '*Krantikarak Rajguru*' (author - Dr. Sachchidanand Shewde), Rajguru, in early March 1929, had left Agra to visit Pune. He stayed there at the residence of Bheema Parkhi but used to take meals at his brother's residence. He showed them his gun and also boasted about the secret revolutionary organization and his role in Saunders' assassination. He also visited the house of his cousin sister, Soutoli Kanade, and recited sacred hymns aloud during meals. This act made an undercover C.I.D. agent, Udhav Rao Pouranik, curious about him and he made enquires about Rajguru from Parkhee. An absolute non-smoker, Rajguru also started to smoke boxes of cigarettes and also became a heavy tobacco consumer.

The book also informs that Rajguru had gone back to Agra from Pune on receiving the information about planning of Assembly bomb case and assault on Viceroy. These statements can not be verified now and it seems highly improbable that Rajguru could have left his colleagues for so long.

Assembly bomb case

The idea of throwing a bomb in the Central Assembly Hall was first perceived by Bhagat Singh, who firmly believed that an act of this magnitude was needed to arouse public awareness on the issue of independence of the nation. The disappointment caused by failure to have Chatterjee released or bomb the train carrying Simon Commission members were only partly compensated by Saunders' assassination. The youth of the nation were restless and the ammunition in the form of bombs was also available with revolutionaries.

The Government had proposed to introduce two repressive bills, namely Public Safety Bill and Trade Disputes Bill. Public Safety Bill was intended to repress the nation-wide youth agitation while Trade Disputes Bill was proposed to provide the Government the powers to take stringent measures to curb even the routine trade union activities. The Viceroy had already hinted that if the bills were not passed in the Assembly, he will have the bills promulgated through Ordinance, using his special powers.

Bhagat Singh, therefore, proposed that a bomb should be thrown from visitor's gallery towards the Treasury benches, just before the declaration of promulgation of the bills by the Viceroy, to show the magnitude of the public displeasure. At the same time, pamphlets showing the protest of HSRA against the unjustifiable provisions of these bills should also be thrown and the Comrades, after doing so, should surrender there and later use the Court as a platform for explaining the purpose of their action. The Central Committee, after long deliberations, approved the idea but still the disputes over the names of the comrades were to be settled.

Since Bhagat Singh had pioneered this idea and he was supposedly the best presenter, being a good orator as well as well qualified in English and socialistic thoughts, he struck the strongest claim. Azad and other colleagues thought otherwise as Bhagat Singh, in their opinion, was the most important member of the group. They settled on Batukeshwar Dutt, who had moved to Bengal as he had become frustrated with the lethargic attitude of the Party. For his accomplice, the names of Ramsharan Das, a 1915 Lahore Conspiracy case convict, Bijoy Kumar Sinha, Jaidev Kapoor and Rajguru were discussed.

The Central committee met a second time, at the instance of Sukhdev and finalized the names of Bhagat Singh and Batukeshwar Dutt. All barring Shiv Verma and Jaidev Kapoor, were ordered to leave Delhi. Azad, too, moved to Jhansi.

Rajguru felt annoyed at being left out because of two reasons. Firstly, he considered Bhagat Singh to be the greatest rival in acts of bravery and secondly, he did not want any opportunity to make supreme sacrifice to slip away from his hands. He was well aware that he would be awarded capital punishment for killing Saunders and never feared it. He could never tolerate to be overtaken by Bhagat Singh on any occasion for sacrifice and expression of love for motherland. The rivalry was intense to such an extent that one might imagine that even on the day of hanging, he would have been worried that Bhagat Singh was not hanged before him. Even on gallows, while suspended, he might have been wondering if Bhagat Singh departs first....

Rajguru visited Jhansi and tried to convince Azad that he was a better candidate than Bhagat Singh for this mission. Azad tried to convince him that he would not be able to deliver the speech in English in Assembly Hall. Rajguru still did not concede, "Is it necessary to deliver speech in English? I can do this in Hindi. If English is all that essential, then I would mug up the whole text and speak without fault. I was able to learn whole of *Laghu Siddantha Koumudi* by heart. Why I, now, am being considered incompetent to read out four pages of English text."

Azad, to shrug him off, scrolled few lines on a piece of paper stating that if Bhagat Singh felt fit then, he could replace Dutt with Rajguru, and asked Rajguru to meet Bhagat Singh in Delhi.

Rajguru met Bhagat Singh and tried very hard to convince him using emotion filled words, " I want to make it very clear that I do not want to lag behind you in the field of sacrifice. My father died when I was a young child. God did not give me good physique or complexion. Don't you agree that you have always surpassed me? Allow me a chance to lead from the front. Secondly, I feel that a vibrant youth like you should work for the party and the nation for some more time. The party will be benefited by your expertise and skills. The party loses nothing by sacrificing me."

These words irritated Bhagat Singh but he also felt moved by the sincerity of the statement. He tried to convince Rajguru that now the Central Committee meeting could not be called to alter the decision as the time was very short. The action was to be taken day after tomorrow and any trivial hindrance could cost dear in its implementation. Rajguru would have his occasion when he would be tried for Saunders' case. The words, however, failed to convince Rajguru and he left the place in great despair.

Regarding his subsequent activities, there are different versions from different authors. According to Bhagwan Das Mahore (in the Book *Yash ki Dharohar*), he left for Pune, saying that he would see as to what can he do now while Shri Krishna Saral (in the book 'Krantikari Shaheed Rajguru'), has narrated that Bhagat Singh was able to convince Rajguru, who returned to his colleagues at Agra. The later version seems to be more authentic as it has been proven that Rajguru, along with Kishorilal, had visited Jhansi on 2nd May, 1929 to meet Azad.

Bhagat Singh and Batukeshwar Dutt exploded the bomb in Central Assembly Hall on 8th April, 1929 and marched in history. Both were shot into the horizon of Indian freedom struggle like stars.

Challenging the crown

The preparations for throwing the bomb in Assembly were going on in full swing. Still, the revolutionaries were filled with the desire of achieving more. They were now quite keen to kill the lion rather than lambs.

The party received the news that on the eve of *Holi*, Viceroy would be attending a dinner along with all I.C.S. Secretaries and pro-government Assembly members. The party, at that time, had all its members and ammunitions readily available, hence the decision to assassinate the Viceroy was made. Azad, too, consented for this action.

Implementation of this plan was no kids play but revolutionaries, with their morale up, seemed not to pay any attention to hurdles. The implementation was entrusted to Shiv Verma, as leader, and Rajguru and Jaidev Kapoor as his accomplices. All three observed the Viceroy several times to make a clear identification so that a wrong person was not killed.

On 25th March, 1929 evening, Shiv Verma, Rajguru and Jaidev Kapoor stationed themselves a short distance away from Vicerical House. Each of them was having two bombs, loaded revolvers and extra cartridge magazine with him.

On the first front, Rajguru was placed to identify the target. He was instructed only to signal, by raising the hand, that Viceroy was in the vehicle. Under no conditions, he was to assault himself. Jaidev Kapoor was next. He was to throw the bomb on Viceroy's vehicle, after receiving the signal. Lastly Shiv Verma was to throw the bomb on Viceroy's vehicle, if Jaidev Kapoor failed to do so.

The Viceroy vehicle was marked by the sign of Crown. It was preceded and followed by a motorcycle rider and lastly, a security van, Rajguru was also made responsible for dealing with security guards. If was decided that all three, after the bomb explosion, would escape and if not able to do so, then would go down fighting.

At the stipulated time, the front motorcycle appeared, moving steadily. Behind him, the Viceroy vehicle, marked with the sign of Crown followed. Rajguru was sure of the identification but made no signal. Shiv Verma and Kapoor were astonished. Then, they saw the inside of the vehicle, now passing in front of them. There were only three ladies and a driver, Viceroy was not in the vehicle. The doubts cleared instantly.

They commended Rajguru for not committing the mistake of making the signal, and thus avoiding unnecessary killing of innocent lives. Azad, too, appreciated his patience. Rajguru, then, related this incident of the murder of Hassan Nizami's father-in-law, which had taught him a great lesson. He further maintained that he would have preferred not to signal even when Viceroy would have been accompanying those three ladies as he thought it improper to kill four innocent people, including the driver, for one person.

Azad immediately remarked. "Three ladies together seem to work some magic over you, each time you encounter them". Rajguru immediately blushed.

Later they learnt that Viceroy had gone to some other place before attending the party and had reached the dinner venue by some other route. The revolutionaries were wise in aborting this attack as an unsuccessful venture might have provided pro-government, so-called soft liners, with an opportunity to criticize them and wish all good things for the Viceroy, as had been after the unsuccessful Viceroy Train blast attempt on December 23rd, 1929. But, if they would have succeeded, then the British might have been forced to leave India long before 1947.

Last meeting with leader

All revolutionaries left Delhi on the orders of their leader, Azad, after Assembly bomb case. The Central Committee also ordered the shifting of headquarters from Agra to Saharanpur. They also rented a house in Lakad Mandi area of Saharanpur on April 2nd, 1929 for this purpose.

Bhagat Singh and Batukeshwar Dutt had already surrendered after exploding the bomb at the Assembly on 8th April 1929. Exactly a week later, on 15th April, the police raided the bomb factory at Kashmiri building, Lahore and arrested Sukhdev, Kishorilal and Jaigopal. Jaigopal turned approver and sang like a canary. This caused great damage to the organization as police was continuously raiding strategic locations to apprehend the revolutionaries.

During this period Rajguru and Savargaonkar stayed at Kashi while Azad moved to Jhansi. From May onwards, the headquarters had virtually shifted to Jhansi.

On 2nd May, many stalwarts, including Bhagwandas, Sadashiv, Vaishampayan, Shiv Verma, Rajguru and Kundanlal, gathered at Azad's residence in Jhansi. They all were talking about Bhagat Singh and Dutt.

Shiv Verma had brought a newspaper having photograph of both the heroes. One colleague, by accident, stepped on the newspaper. Seeing that, Azad suddenly burst with anger but he immediately controlled his emotions and said. "These are now the national treasure and will be worshipped after achieving martyrdom. They, now, rank far above us and therefore, stepping on their photographs will amount to crushing the national pride.

Shiv Verma, then, started discussing the prospects of throwing the bomb on Viceroy at Dehradun and seeking the forced release of Bhagat Singh and Dutt on the way from Delhi to Lahore. Rajguru also participated in the discussion till late afternoon, then he and Kundanlal retired for some rest.

Azad, by now quite emotional, straightway ruled out the attack on Viceroy with the words. "I will not risk my colleagues for such missions. It is not proper for me being the team leader to gather new colleagues, throw them in fire and then sit comfortably to get newer ones."

That very day, Surendra Nath Pandey joined them from Indore. He had come with the information that police had learnt about Azad's location at Jhansi and Shambhunath, C.I.D. Inspector from Kanpur, on his trail, had already arrived in Jhansi. The police was likely to raid several places in Jhansi during the night.

At that time, all colleagues, excluding Vaishampayan, were present there. It was not safe for them all to leave *en masse* during the dark of the night. They requested Azad to leave at once. Azad dismissed the idea and used his master card. "Being the team leader, I order the four of you to leave this place one by one and leave Jhansi immediately." He kept only Bhagwandas and Sadashiv with him.

Other colleagues had no option but to comply. As decided by Azad, Shiv Verma followed by Rajguru Pandey and Kundanlal left the house one by one. They all walked for some distance and then joined together. After some time, the police raided the house with heavy arrangements. But, by this time, Azad and both of his colleagues, too had deserted the house and left for some unknown destination. The police could recover only few broken earthen utensils and old newspapers.

This was to be the last meeting between the two great warriors, Azad and Rajguru.

Final journey begins

Within next few days, the events took such a rapid paced, which served to create visible cracks in the entire organizational infrastructure. The arrest of Bhagat Singh and Dutt in Assembly bomb case on 7th April 1929 was followed by successful raid on Lahore bomb factory, a week later, on 15th April resulting in the arrest of Sukhdev, Kishorilal and Jaigopal. Next month, the scene turned even gloomier with arrest of Hansraj Vohra at Lahore on 2nd May and raid on Saharanpur bomb factory on 13th May. Fanindra Nath Ghosh was arrested on 8th June at Calcutta and Man Mohan Banerjee on 16th June. The biggest jolt, which shattered the whole organisation, was received when Jaigopal, Hansraj Vohra, Ghosh and Banerjee turned approver and disclosed all the secret information.

At that time, Rajguru and Savargaonkar were staying at Kashi. Little information is available, which is now difficult to trace after lapse of 80 years, about as to how and when they moved to Pune. From the analysis of memoirs, narrated by colleague Shiv Verma in his book "Sansmratiyan", Marathi laureate Vishnoo Shridhar Joshi in his book "Wadnawal" and his childhood friend Dattatreya Balwant Karandikar (PW 416 in Lahore Conspiracy Case), the following picture emerges.

When the turbulence started, both, Rajguru and Savargaonkar, clandestinely moved from Kashi to

Amravati. He joined the summer camp at the gymnasium, maintained by *Hanuman Prasarak Mandal* to continue his exercises. He started motivating youth in nationalistic ideology. He abruptly left the place one day as he suspected the presence of detectives among the followers.

Both then reached Akola and started living in a room near Raj Rajeshwar Temple, arranged by Bapu Saheb Sahstrabuddhe. Few days later, they kept moving between Amrawati, Nagpur and Wardha with the aim of recruiting youth for revolution.

During this period he stayed with one of the *Rashtriya Swayam Sewak* Sangh workers, and through him also met Dr. Keshav Baliram Hedgewar, the Founder President of R.S.S. According to the book, authored by Shri Krishna Saral, he also took asylum at Ujjain for few days, at the residence of his childhood friend, Ram Chandra Karnawat. Rajguru, in the meantime, had communicated his intentions of strengthening the organization in Maharashtra. Azad sent Vaishampayan for his assistance in this task. Bhagwandas Mahore, in his book *Yash ki Dharohar*, has also mentioned about his activities in Maharashtra.

The proceedings against Bhagat Singh and Dutt in Assembly bomb case had already started in Sessions Court, while Rajguru was in Akola. Both, Jaigopal and Hans Raj Vohra, now government approvers, disclosed to the police about the involvement of a Maratha youth, code named 'M' in Saunders' assassination. The police now started searching for him in Maharashtra too. He then moved on towards Mumbai, but, according to a set plan, left the vehicle at a very small place on Mumbai-Deccan highway. During the night, a truck stopped at the place. There was exchange of signals and then Rajguru

He along with Savargaonkar, started training youth in revolutionary ideology at Maharashtra *Mandal* gymnasium. He also started exercising and amazed the public with his skills in exercising, shooting and fighting with lathi. But his aggressive teaching style alerted the gymnasium management, as this could spell trouble for them. Sensing this, Rajguru himself stopped visiting the facility.

He was not the type of person who could stay in peace. He started planning to assassinate sir Ledericks Sykes, the Governor of Bombay. He communicated the idea to Azad through Vaishampayan and got his liberal approval. Azad sent Bhagwandas and Sadashiv from Gwalior to Pune with two guns, two bombs, cartridges and raw material for making bombs. To change the train, both got down at Bhusawal. Due to lack of coordination, both got apprehended by excise police at railway station and were sent to Jalgaon Jail. Rajguru could learn it only through newspapers.

Next day, Rajguru and Savargaonkar were to learn the demoralizing news of passing away of Yateendra Nath Das alias Jatin Babu following prolonged hunger strike at Lahore. The great martyr refused to bow before the tyrannical Government and earned respect from Hamilton, the Superintendent of Police, Lahore and the Court, posthumously. The news further lowered their spirits.

In the meantime, Rajguru came in contact with Sharad Keskar, nephew of a renowned Congress leader. In reality Keskar was a police informer and had been recruited by the intelligence to keep a trail on Rajguru. Keskar told him that being proficient in the lathi work, he could make pistol parts. Savargaonkar had no idea about Keskar. Rajguru, in good faith, discussed many plans

The Tribune.

VOL. LI. NO. 70 LAHORE, WEDNESDAY, MARCH 25, 1931. Price One Anna

BHAGAT SINGH, RAJGURU AND SUKHDEV EXECUTED.

NO "LAST INTERVIEW" WITH RELATIONS.

Shouts Emerge From Jail.

DEAD BODIES SECRETLY DISPOSED OF

Removed to Distant Place.

Thick Veil of Secrecy.

Relations' Futile Quest for Dead Bodies.

Bhagat Singh's Letter.

TRUCE TERMS NOT BEING CARRIED OUT.

Congressmen's Feeling.

TWISTED WRECKAGE OF ROYAL SCOT

Fastest Train in World

DEAD BODIES WRAPPED.

Not Given to Relations

Optical Instruments

The Front Page of the Tribune newspaper with news of execution of Bhagat Singh, Rajguru and Sukhdev

D.A.V. College, Kanpur

Varanasi School

with Keskar, without being aware of the lurking danger, this fellow was going to make him face.

On 27th September 1929, Shivram Paranjape, Editor-Publisher of the news letter 'Kal' and an associate of revolutionaries, died at Pune. Next day, his funeral procession started from Tilak Bagh. Rajguru attended the procession and with great enthusiasm, deliberately shouted the slogans "Long Live Revolution" and "Down with the imperialism". This was sufficient to arouse suspicion among the intelligence officers, who were keeping a watch over the proceedings, as the slogans were the ones shouted by Lahore Conspiracy case under-trials.

Rajguru was eager to kill the Bombay Governor. Keskar informed him about the Governor's visit to Race Course to attend a function related to Governor's Cup. Keskar, the traitor, was already under control of Holland, D.I.G., C.I.D., Bombay through Kavthalkar, the local C.I.D. Officer. On Holland's orders, the Lahore Police escorted Jai Gopal to Race Course, Pune, while keeping his face under the veil.

Rajguru, totally unaware of the conspiracy, returned from the funeral and after taking bath, left for the Race Course alone, without even informing Savargaonkar. The place was amidst heavy police security and Rajguru was unable to penetrate it. He was very much disappointed at the missed opportunity of killing the Governor. Keskar and Kavthalkar, however, were overjoyed as Jai Gopal identified Rajguru correctly. The police did not attempt to apprehend him in Race Course as being armed, he could have had an opportunity to escape. They decided to arrest him with all precautions.

A dejected Rajguru walked back and informed Savargaonkar about the failed mission. Savargaonkar warned him about keeping distance from Keskar as he was not fully confident about him.

On 29th September 1929, a Pune cinema theatre was showing the documentary on the funeral procession of Jatin Babu. Rajguru and Savargaonkar viewed the last glimpses of their departed colleagues in the matinee show and were back home at 6 p.m. Both kept discussing over the days spent with Jatin Babu at Lahore and Agra. They went to Dinkar's residence for dinner and returned again at around 8 p.m.

At 8 p.m. Keskar and Karandikar visited the room and Keskar produced a broken gun. Savargaonkar was not interested and returned the weapon. Then Keskar, with glowing eyes, examined the six rounds gun, shown by Rajguru. After Keskar was gone, Savargaonkar once again tried to convince Rajguru that this fellow was not trustworthy as he was boasting about having access to a gun factory. Rajguru dismissed his pleadings with a smile.

Keskar, upon return, immediately contacted Kavthalkar, the C.I.D. Inspector and Fouzdar Lugade and gave the signal.

Since it was quite late, both friends put out the lamp and were instantly fast asleep. As was jocularly forecasted, Rajguru was nearing the arrest, while sleeping.

At about 1 a.m. Savargaonkar heard some sounds of steps over the staircase. Thinking that some friend had arrived, he opened the door and peeped outside. Suddenly the hell broke loose. The room was stormed by a sergeant, accompanied by six constables. More policemen followed, now totaling twelve. Before they could understand the scene and reach for the weapons, they were forcibly rendered immobile and handcuffed.

Syed Ahmed Shah, Dy. S.P. C.I.D. Special Staff, Lahore, had himself arrived at Pune to make this arrest. He deposed before the Lahore conspiracy case Tribunal (PW 411 on 15th and 16th August 1930) that he, after reaching Pune, had arrested Rajguru, along with one other person, while sleeping. He also mentioned about recovery of a tin box from Rajguru, which contained a revolver and 14 cartridges. Inspector E. Mills of Pune City Police Station (PW 413) supported him by submitting that following instructions from Holland, D.I.G., C.I.D., Rajguru and Savargaonkar were arrested from plot number 20, Tilak Road, Pune City in the presence of Syed Ahmed Shah, Dy. S.P. and a revolver, thirteen 0.45 bore and one 0.38 bore cartridges were seized from them. Jaswant Rai Sawant (PW 415) and Khwaza Tajuddin, Inspector, C.I.D. Special Staff, Punjab also made similar depositions.

Both were handcuffed and taken downstairs. A large crowd had already gathered. They, on sighting the crowd, started shouting the slogans "Long Live Revolution" and "Down with imperialism". This made the crowd learn that the persons arrested were revolutionaries. Both were then taken to Farashkhana Police out post, amidst heavy slogan shouting. On being asked their names by the Police, Rajguru declined to tell his name.

That very night, Police raided the home of Dattatreya Balwant Karandikar, his childhood friend, situated at House number 170, Shakkar Peth, Pune City and seized one revolver and 15 cartridges from his custody. They also seized a fully loaded automatic revolver from a coat pocket found hanging in the motor garage. Karandikar (PW 416) later deposed before the tribunal that all the seized articles belonged to Rajguru, who had given these to him for making repairs. Actually, Rajguru had already briefed Karandikar to inform police, in event of seizure, that the articles belonged to him. Due to this, Karandikar was sentenced to one year rigorous imprisonment by Poona Court under section 19(f) of the Arms Act.

Next day, on 1st October, Shivram Hari Rajguru's identification was confirmed by his brother, Dinkar. The police found a Benaras postal receipt in his name from Dinkar's house on search.

Inspector Mills, at Borstal Institute, asked Rajguru to record his thumb and finger prints. Rajguru had not yet lost his sense of humour and said, "I will not commit myself. You can have them only by using force. The police could restrain him after a lot of effort and then only, recording could be done.

In the meantime, Uddhav Rao Pouranik reached there and, on sighting Rajguru , instantly asked him, "Hey, Bapu Saheb. How come you are here? What is your crime? Do you need any help?" This was a God sent opportunity for Police as they had a second identifier. The formalities were completed quickly and both were now to be taken to Lahore.

The gallant Maratha made the final bow to his birth place and prepared to begin his journey towards the final abode. Both were now being taken to Lahore, under the alert vigil of Syed Ahmed Shah.

The ordeal

Lahore Police escorted Rajguru and Savargaonkar from Pune to Lahore via Kalyan. At Lahore, Bhagat Singh and other colleagues were on hunger strike inside the Jail. To feel associated with them, both, too, stopped taking meals right from the start of the journey.

The news about their arrest had already spread like wildfire throughout the country by the newspapers. The people flocked together in hundreds and thousands at all stations to have a glimpse of their heroes. Rajguru and Savargaonkar, despite being without meals, greeted them with patriotic slogans, followed by similar echoes from the crowd.

At Ashok Nagar Railway Station (of the then Gwalior State, now in Madhya Pradesh), almost the whole population gathered. Rajguru, as usual, peeped out, while shouting slogans. An arrogant British officer struck him with a cane. That made the blood of an 11 year old child boil. In the spur of the moment, he picked up a stone and pelted. The officer was injured. Then all police men, began mercilessly beating him, causing serious injuries. That moment, a living legend was born.

This boy's name was Shri Krishna Saral, later widely known as the 'Living Martyr, as he went on to author more than 125 books, including 12 epics, on Indian revolutionaries. He sold all his property to traval throughout India and twelve other countries to collect authentic information about the history of revolution in India and communicate the *gathas* to the public. He also wrote a short treatise on Rajguru. The release of his epic on Bhagat Singh in 1964 at Ujjain was attended by the great martyr's mother, Smt. Vidyavati, herself.

They finally reached Lahore. On 3rd October 1929, Inspector Deena Nath Bakshi (PW 6) took Rajguru to the residence of Rai Saheb Pt. Shri Krishna, Special Magistrate, Lahore Cantt. for seeking police remand. The Magistrate jokingly asked, "Your name is Rajguru, but your acts are quite contrary to your name." Rajguru could never be bowed down. He instantly remarked. "Yes, My name is Rajguru (the royal teacher) and my job is to teach lesson to the rulers."

Rajguru, on police remand, was kept at Kotvali, Lahore and he felt bad at being kept isolated from his colleagues.

On 4th October, Choudhry Mushtaq Ahmed, Magistrate Class I, took him to the Old Fort, Lahore where approvers Fanindra Nath Ghosh, Jai Gopal, Hansraj Vohra and Lalit Kumar Mukherjee confirmed his identification.

On 5th October, Rajguru and Savargaonkar, on receiving the news of ending of hunger strike by their colleagues, took the meals after five days.

On 6th October, Choudhry Mushtaq Ahmed, took him, face hidden under a veil, to the Old Fort, Lahore for identification parade. Hussain Bakhsh, Buddhu, Fakirchand and Boora identified Rajguru as a visitor in the Irene Building, Mozang House. Shobhram recognized him as the person seen at the house owned by Parvati Devi in Gwal Mandi, Lahore but Parvati Devi herself, failed to identify him. Noor Mohammad recognized him as a person frequenting Seetaram Bazaar, Delhi. The eye witnesses, Fakir Chand and Constable Mohammed Ibrahim identified him as the person who fired at Saunders while Ata Mohammed, Aftab Ahmed, Ghotama, Chhotu Singh and of all people, Ferns, the traffic inspector who was attacked by Rajguru, failed to make a correct recognition.

The identification parade continued on 7th October also in front of Choudhry Mushaq Ahmed. Mohammed Irshad Ali and Abdul Aziz Beg identified him as the person residing at Hing ki Mandi, Agra in the house rented by Bharosilal. Gendamal recognized him as the one frequenting the house of Jwala Prasad at Noorie Gate, Agra while Beni Prasad, milk vendor at the same place, identified him as one of his customers. The sweeper Gama confirmed his presence at the Irene Building, Lahore, along with other youth. Ramsharan Das identified him as the person who had stayed in his hotel at Firozepur for three days during the last winters. However, Ajmer Singh, Choudhary Kamaldeen, Gurubachan Singh, Ram Swarup,Narendra Prasad, Jwala Prasad, Bharosilali and Abdul Jabbar failed to recognize him.

At the same time he was being subjected to heavy torture by the police for extraction of vital information of the party and his colleagues. Savargaonkar was neither recognized by any of the witnesses nor connected to the Lahore Conspiracy case. The Police sent him back to Pune, where he was kept at Yerwada Jail for being an accomplice of Rajguru.

On 10th October, the parade continued in front of Choudhary Roshanlal, Magistrate. The witness Abdulla identified him, while Gendalal, after faltering once, made the identification after being tutored by police.

On 15th October, Choudhary Mushtaq Ahmed again conducted the identification parade at Old Fort. Ram Prasad, a shopkeeper at Gwal Mandi, Lahore. identified him as the one who visited Parvatibai's residence last winters. Ramdulare, from Jhansi, recollected that Rajguru had visited him twice, once alone and once with Pandit Ramsahay. He also informed that, once, Sadashiv and Panditji had visited his house to meet Rajguru. Somnath, too, made a correct identification but Avinash Chander, Mohammed Nazeer, Ganga Bisen and Heeralal failed to identify him.

The trial for Lahore Conspiracy case was being conducted in the Court of Rai Saheb Pandit Shri Krishna, Special Magistrate, located in a spacious barrack in the southern corner of the perimeter of Central Jail, Lahore. Rajguru made his first appearance in the court on 17th October 1919. He was very much thrilled and excited at the thought of joining his friends. While taking the first step inside, he shouted "Inquilab Zindabad", which was reciprocated by a chorus of cheers echoing throughout the Court. They quickly started embracing each other warmly.

His entry brought a fresh vigour to his colleagues. The void created by the death of Yatindranath Das seemed to get filled. Later Pandit Shri Krishna, while deposing before the tribunal, mentioned that after his entry in the court, Rajpguru and his colleagues had greeted each other warmly.

On 18th October, he was sent to the Borstal Jail and became his usual self on joining the old band.

On 19th October, Netaji Subhas Chandra Bose, the great Congress leader, came to the court to meet the under-trials. He was first detained at the jail gates for more than one hour, subjected to search and then, finally denied interview with revolutionaries by the Magistrate, even after sitting in the Court for three hours. Kiran, brother of martyr Yatindranath was denied access inside. Bhagat Singh raised the issue of discriminatory behaviour with Indians and the Court acting as a puppet of the Government and the police before the Magistrate, but even the heated arguments could not move the Court.

Newspapers were disseminating all the news among general public, which was beginning to wake up against the oppressive actions of the Government. The revolutionaries, as a matter of policy, were contesting the case and staking their lives for public awareness rather then for defense. The Government made all efforts to segregate revolutionaries from the public, but the smarter heroes used the court itself for publicizing their aims and objectives, and thus making the desired impact over peoples' minds.

They used to enter the courts like gladiators entering the arena. Their confident actions and gazes used to stimulate the audience very much. They walked inside the court amidst heavy patriotic slogan shouting, which shook even the most dormant minds. 'Inquilab Zindabad' induced a desire for making self-sacrifice while "Vande Mataram' aroused the patriotic feelings in everybody's mind. These fanatics used to recite:

Sarfaroshi ki tamanna ab hamare dil mein hai,
Dekhna hai zor kitna baazuae quatil mein hai.

(Our heart is lit by the desire of sacrifice; now we have to measure the power of the assassin.)

They also popularized the memorable lines from great poet, Om Prakash:

Kabhi voh bhi din aayega, hum aazad honge,
Yeh apni zamin hogi, yeh apna aasman hoga;
Shaheedon ki chitaaon par lagenge har baras mele,
Watan par marne walon ka baki yahi nishan hoga.

(A day will come, when we shall be independent; This will be our own land and own sky; there will be fairs at the funeral pyres of the martyrs; that will be the only sign left of those sacrificing themselves for the nation).

There was invariably a large gathering outside the court. The public used to join the chorus. The court, annoyed by this, passed an order banning slogan making inside the court, over which the defense lawyer, Lala Dunichand, immediately raised an objection.

Jaigopal, the traitor turned approver, appeared in the court on 21st October 1929, instead of having expression of guilt on face, he exuded an air of arrogance and sarcasm. All the accused greeted him with shouts of "Shame! Shame!" Premchand, youngest of them all, could not contain himself and hurled a slipper towards the traitor. The Court immediately ordered handcuffing of all the accused, while in court. There was a lot of turmoil, leading to suspension of the proceedings. Premchand was sentenced to three months for this offence.

After returning to the jail, the three member committee comprising of Bhagat Singh, Sukhdev and Vijay Kumar Sinha, decided to boycott the court proceedings, unless the Magistrate withdrew the order regarding handcuffing the prisoners. Next day, they refused to attend the Court. The police could manage to get only a few prisoners inside the van. As the van reached from Borstal Jail to Central Jail, they arranged themselves in interlaced web, which could not be penetrated by even the massively deployed police.

Next day, police promised them to take off the handcuffs upon reaching the Court but did not fulfill it. The handcuffs were taken off only during the lunch, and after that, all accused refused to be handcuffed again. The Magistrate had anticipated this and asked police to teach them a good lesson. Bhagat Singh and Rajguru, among all, received the worst treatment. There were heated scuffles between both sides. Bhagat Singh in great anger asked the Magistrate, "Have you really ordered the police to turn brutal? Now you can not restrain them. Is this what you call decent behavior?"

They were given the more severe treatment inside the jail too but declined to yield. The news leaked outside through public visitors present inside. The police atrocity was condemned in a public protest meeting at Lahore. Next day, all national dailies, including those from London, published this news on their front page. The Magistrate was forced to retract his draconian order regarding handcuffing.

Rajguru was not the type of person who could bow down before tyranny and he was usually the first one to express himself freely. During an imbroglio, he was always on the front line. He and Mahaveer Singh, once, lost consciousness during the merciless beating of fifteen odd unarmed prisoners by more than 300 armed police men at the Jail gate on 25th October.

Many great leaders of national fame, including Subhas Chandra Bose, Baba Gurditt Singh, K.F. Nariman, the King of Kalakanker, Rafi Ahmed Kidwai, Mohanlal Saxena and Pandit Motilal Nehru, attended the Court at many times to boost the morale of the revolutionaries. Nehru attended the Court twice and on 29th December 1929, he spent an hour with the accused.

Rajguru, like other colleagues, was also using the Court as a platform for voicing the selfless revolutionary ideology and patriotism, but he also used the court to reveal his humorous nature. The voicing was mainly entrusted to Bhagat Singh, serving as their chief spokesperson. Rajguru had no interest in the proceedings of the court or examination of witness, but always derived great pleasure in teasing the officers with his mischievous nature.

He demanded for a Marathi interpreter to assist him in the Court, pleading his inability to speak or understand English and Hindi. To prove, that Rajguru was well conversant in Hindi, the Government arranged, at its expense, the deposition of a Kashi resident in the Court to this effect.

His colleague Kashiram narrated an interesting story. He visited revolutionaries in the Court in December 1929. The Court proceedings had been suspended due to non-cooperation of the accused. All colleagues, in lighter vein, were going near Kashiram, saluting him and getting some edibles. Rajguru, all a sudden, started speaking aloud in fluent English about Kashiram extending special favour to Jaidev, by gifting him pen and shawl. Rajguru in a jovial mood after seeing Kashiram after about one and half years, forgot his disguise and continued to talk in English. Niaz Ahmed, C.I.D. Officer from Punjab Police, was standing nearby and noted his eloquence and chided Kashiram that he should be ready to depose on oath regarding Rajguru's knowledge of Hindi and English.

Rajguru devised yet another trick. He started muttering continuously in the Court, the pitch of the murmur increasing during the proceedings. When the magistrate tried to stop him, he, with an innocent face, said, "What can I do? I am unable to comprehend what is being spoken here. I can not cross-examine the witness as no interpreter has been provided to me. In these circumstances, I can not do anything but grumble."

On 4th January 1930, Bhagat Singh presented an application on behalf of Rajguru, seeking information about the order passed by the Court, on Rajguru's petition to interview his attorney, Dr. Hardikar. Magistrate informed that it had been forwarded to the jail authorities. Bhagat Singh had then raised objection over this illegal procedure. This news was published in 'The Tribune', January 5th, 1930 issue.

The deliberate manipulation of the Court by the revolutionaries to disseminate their messages was causing delay in proceedings. Annoyed by this, the prosecution submitted a petition before the Lahore High Court under Section 561-A of the Criminal Procedure Code, to issue appropriate orders, using its inherent powers, for completing the initial investigation summarily for the case to be made over to higher Court.

The petition was heard by Chief Justice Shadilal and Justice Broadway on 7th January 1930. According to the news published in 'The Tribune', January 8th, 1930 issue, the accused were brought in the Court under heavy police arrangements, No one, barring the lawyers, was allowed inside the Court room. Even the lawyers could enter only after being searched. Bhagat Singh and Dutt pleaded and argued upon the case themselves. Rajguru continued his drama here too. He started muttering in Marathi, when the Public Prosecutor Conrod Noad was in argument with Amardas and Sant Singh. On being informed about his inability to understand Hindi and English, the Court appointed an interpreter for him. The petition was dismissed by the Honourable Court on 31st January

1930. This Judgment has been published in the journals as "Crown vs. Sukhdev and Anr. AIR 1930, Lahore 465.

A defense committee had been formed to contest the case. The committee received financial contributions from all over the county and abroad. Many senior Lahore advocates had volunteered to appear for accused free of cost, but, as mentioned earlier, defense was the priority for revolutionaries. Senior Barrister, Lala Dunichand used to appear as the legal counsel for Bhagat Singh. On basis of the objections raised by the public prosecutor, the court refused to permit Lala Dunichand inside the court in any capacity, neither for defense, nor as member of the Bar nor as a visitor in press gallery and asked him to leave. Opposing this humiliating act, the revolutionaries decided to boycott the court from 29th January 1930.

The revolutionaries were being deprived of the opportunity to be heard as they were being denied interview with their relatives and legal advisors. The sub-human treatment by police was another concern. Bhagat Singh wrote to the Court, "We resent the drama being played in the name of justice. We are denied all opportunities to defend ourselves. The under-trials are not to be treated as convict. We will attend the court, only when our grievances are removed."

The revolutionaries had ended their previous hunger strike on 5th October 1929, responding to government's promise for provision of better behavior, food and other facilities. As the government went back on its assurances, the revolutionaries resumed their second hunger strike. Rajguru had not been there on previous episode, so he felt especially thrilled at this opportunity of making a sacrifice.

Rajguru, at the time of admission in the jail, was 126 pounds. In a letter written in Marathi to his family, he had promised to inform about his weight gain. By 13th day of hunger strike, his weight came down to 105 pounds and the fall continued. He took hardly a cup of water in two days. Dehydration had led to extreme weakness, swelling of the face, bad taste in mouth and halitosis was not relieved even after brushing thrice. Later, he was only gargling instead of drinking water. There was bleeding in his throat and nose.

The doctors selected the worst affected ones, including Rajguru, for forced feeding on thirteenth day. They, as had happened with Yateendranath Das on previous episode, placed the feeding tube accidentally in bronchi in stead of stomach and introduced the milk. This caused pneumonia as a result of severe lung infection. He still managed to write the word 'Success' on a slip and gave it to Shiv Verma. Despite being seriously ill, his courage was commendable.

Following excerpts from the Rajguru's medical report, mentioned on certified copies and pages number 12, 13 and 18 of Home Political Department File No. O-36/III/1930'reports on the health and treatment of prisoner in Lahore Conspiracy Case, received from National Archives, New Delhi serve to provide a glimpse of his condition during and after the hunger strike:

19th February 1930-Prisoner Shiv Ram Rajguru-Temperature M 100/E 101, Pulse is 80 pm, Respiration is 40 pm, still complains of pain in chest on deep breathing, refuses to take medicine or nourishment, is taking only plain water, owing to pneumonia and lack of nourishment, he is growing weak. His condition should be still considered serious.

21st February 1930-Condition of under-trial Shiv Ram Rajguru-Temperature M 100-R 101. Pulse is 84 pm. Respiration is 40 pm. Examination reveals further extension of pneumonia in both the lungs. He is taking medicines and nourishments ordered for him. General condition poor, all arrangemnts for proper nursing made. He should still be considered seriously. All other under-trials are taking their foods voluntarily and their condition is satisfactory.

Lahore edition of "The Tribune' also published the news on 19th February 1950, that Rajguru was the worst affected among all hunger strikers was virtually on death bed. He was reduced to a skeleton and his lungs were infected leading to fever and he could even barely move on his bed.

The Governor of Punjab forwarded a telegram numered 269 to the Viceroy of India on 18th February, 1930. This stated that Lahore Conspiracy case accused were not in good condition. Out of them, nine accused put up a stiff resistance to forced feeding and any such attempt might result in complications. Four of them were in critical stage and one of them, Rajguru, had turned very weak due to associated pneumonia. It was therefore, necessary to issue orders for revisions in jail manual at the earliest. He believed that such gesture would help the government to favourably manipulate the public opinion, though not specifically useful to these youth. Death due to hunger strike would adversely affect the law and order, leading to dire consequences. In addition, this step would help in speeding up the case too.

Lord Irvin, the Viceroy, sent a telegram R. Number 576.B to the Secretary of State for India, London, next day stating that procedure of forced feeding to nine uncooperative accused could be dangerous. One of them, Rajguru was critically ill. Looking at the increasing public pressure, he also suggested amendments in Jail Manual. The very day, the Government issued the orders regarding changes in the Jail Manual.

The news of likelihood of Rajguru's martyrdom due to hunger strike had already made headlines. This initiated a series of nationwide protests, forcing administration to take urgent decisions. The Government finally yielded to some of the demands made by the revolutionaries.

Deshpande, the interpreter provided to Rajguru in the Court of the Special Magistrate, communicated this news to Baburao Bhatwadekar, a Pune descendent and a chemist in the Railway laboratory. He had come to Lahore in 1927 and was residing at Shiv Niwas, the house owned by Bhagwati Charan. Bhatwadekar had no idea about Rajguru's whereabouts in Pune, but he managed to send a telegram to his family through Kesri, a Pune based newspaper. The defense committee also forwarded some cash to cover travelling expenses.

Dinkar was not tempted to visit Lahore but mother Parvati Devi, despite her bad asthamatic status, expressed her willingness to see her ailing son. It is really suprising to observe lack of affection on part of Dinkar, despite Rajguru spending more than one and a half years in prison, that too when the public was keenly following this trial. Probably the charm of the Government service superseded the love for his brother. But mother Parvati Devi and sister Godawari knew no such fear. They visited Lahore frequently and stayed with Bhagat Singh's family for many days at Khawasarian, near Lahore, during the days preceding the hanging.

Bhatwadekar, despite being a government servant, showed enormous courage in welcoming the two ladies in his home. The permission to meet Rajguru was taken.

Travesty of the judicial system

The case had proceeded in the Court of Special Magistrate at a snail's pace. Only 228 out of 607 witnesses had been examined during eight months. After this, the case was to be decided in the Session Court, after being made over by the subordinate Court, in the presence of Jury and Assessors. Thereafter, there was provision for rights of appeal in High Court and Privy Council.

A lengthy legal procedure, coupled with deliberate use of Courts by revolutionaries for manipulating public opinion, had turned out to be a big headache for the Government. The revolutionaries had been successful in using court for disseminating their ideology and zeal for patriotism among the public and creating a sense of hatred towards British and earned sympathy, affection and respect as national heroes. The terrified Government wanted to get rid of this problem as quickly as possible, but also desired to accomplish it within legal ambit.

The Government introduced a bill on 12th September, 1929 in the Central Assembly seeking rights for judges to continue proceedings, even in the absence of the accused due to any reason. This could not be passed due to severe opposition from Pandit Motilal Nehru, Leader of the Opposition, M.A. Jinnah and gross public unrest. There were, however, hints of using special powers by the Government.

Finally, on 1st May 1930, Lord Irwin, the Viceroy, as Governor General of India, using powers given under Section 72 of Government of India Act, 1915, showing the emergency for better governance in British-ruled India, promulgated the Ordinance of 1930 to try the accused of Lahore Conspiracy Case. The Tribunal formed under this Ordinance had been delegated with greater dictatorial powers than the one formed in 1919 in Jalianwala Bagh Case.

The Tribunal comprised of a President and two members, all judges of Lahore High Court. The case was withdrawn from the purview of the Magistrate and handed over to the Tribunal, without necessitating any commitment process. This was treated at par with the Sessions Court, but following the warrant procedure. One of the most important thing was that the verdict passed by the Tribunal was final. It was competent to award any sentence, including the death sentence, which was not required to be confirmed and no appeal could be filed against the verdict passed by the Tribunal in High Court or any other Court.

The Tribunal was empowered to continue proceedings in absence of the accused, if the accused failed to appear in the Court or resisted efforts to bring them to the Court or caused serious obstruction to the proceedings. The Tribunal could utilize the depositions made by witnesses in the court of the Magistrate or any other court. The Tribunal was also empowered to pass any orders, it considered proper, for the conduct of the trial and any such order could not be challenged in the High Court by way of appeal, revision or any other legal procedure.

The Punjab High Court, Lahore, named Justice J. Coldstream, I.C.S. as the President of the Tribunal and

Justice Agha Hyder, Bar-at-Law and Justice G.C. Hilton as its members. The Government, by forming this Tribunal, intended to provoke the accused to boycott the proceedings for ill-treatment, so that the case could be concluded speedily. The revolutionaries regarded this as a repressive measure but still considered this as a moral victory. The Government had revealed its true intentions through promulgation of this Ordinance and therefore the goal of exposing the Government had been achieved. They also hoped that sleeping population would now wake up after seeing the malicious and atrocious attitude of the Tribunal.

The Poonchh House, Lahore, a palace owned by King of Patiala, had been selected as the office of Tribunal. This occupied the centre stage and was put under heavy police security. The armed police marched everywhere, terrifying people from entering the premises. The C.I.D. had been put on maximum alert as there was information regarding attempt for seeking forced release of the accused. Police was interrogating all suspected person and had arrested over 200 persons on the suspicion of them being sympathizers of the revolutionaries. A limited number of entry passes were issued and hardly thirty to forty persons entered the Court Room on 5th May 1930.

The members entered the room at exactly 10 a.m. and occupied the chairs, with a photograph of George V hanging on the wall behind them. The Government was represented by C.H. Conrod Noad, the Public Prosecutor, K.S. Khalandar Ali Khan, Government Advocate. L. Gopal Lal, Advocate and Bakhshi Deenanath, Prosecuting Police Inspector.

Bhagat Singh, along with 17 other accused, entered the court room at 10.02 a.m. amidst heavy shouts of slogans 'Inquilab Zindabad'. They immediately started singing:

Sarfaroshi ki tamanna ab hamare dil mein hai,
Dekhna hai zor kitna baazuae quatil mein hai.
Waqt aane de bata denge tujhe a-e aasman,
Hum abhi se kya batayen kya hamare dil mein hain.

(Our heart is lit by the desire of sacrifice; now we have to measure the power of the assassin. We shall inform you at the proper time; At this moment we can not tell you what we intend to do).

Justice Coldstream instructed Advocate Gopal Lal to produce an authentic translation of the song before the Tribunal. Justice Agha Hyder, the only Indian Judge in the Tribunal, tried to explain the meaning of the song, but the heavy shouting inside the room rendered it inaudible.

Most historians covering this case have put stress on the written and oral citations made by Bhagat Singh before the Tribunal, ignoring the other accused. Bhagat Singh's role in this case was absolutely vital but the revolutionary, who first attacked the formation of this Tribunal, was none other than Rajguru. The author was priviledged to get a certified copy of the 'Proceeding Book of the Lahore Conspiracy Case, 1930', which was presented to National Archives, New Delhi by Mathura Prasad Thapar, brother of martyr Sukhdev. In this, Rajguru's name gets the mention on the very first page itself.

Rajguru faced the Judges boldly. Challenging the Ordinance, he called the tribunal as unlawfully formed. He stressed upon the argument that the Viceroy, in normal times, did not have the power to cut short the legal process. The Court, therefore, was requested to stop proceedings till the decision on whether the Viceroy had the power to exercise extraordinary powers during normal times.

This complex legal question raised by Rajguru before the court, itself, is sufficient to convince us of his intelligence and knowledge of law. Bhagat Singh and other colleagues supported him but the Tribunal declined to suspend the proceedings refusing to consider this point.

The dual had begun right at the start. The Tribunal was determined to decline all objections raised by the accused while the revolutionaries, too, were determined to use this platform, as they had done in Magistrate Court, to popularize their ideology. They once again started raising slogans.

Rajguru was once again on the front. He started giving speech in Marathi, "The British are blood suckers and have rendered India poor and helpless. You may call this a Government, but it is controlled by only a few privileged ones." The President stopped Rajguru and told him that the Tribunal could not comprehend the language, he was speaking. Rajguru too blurted directly that he, too, did not understand the English language, used in the court and therefore, needed an interpreter. He also submitted a written application to this effect. Noad, the Public Prosecutor, raised the objection on the ground that Rajguru could follow the language used in the court. The court overruled the objection and ordered the appointment of an interpreter. Vasudev, a Pune resident and now a clerk in the Military Accounts Office, Lahore, who was proficient in English, Urdu and Marathi languages, was administered oath and appointed as an interpreter.

On the same day, the Public Prosecutor opened the case for the Government and briefed about the allegations made against the accused. Few accused were declared as absconding. G.P. Hamilton, the S.S.P., Lahore was examined as first witness by the prosecution, followed by the approver Jai Gopal.

On 6th May 1930, the Tribunal asked each of the accused whether he wanted to be represented by a Counsel at Government's expense. Most of the accused declined to engage the counsel or preferred not to reply to any question. Rajguru, too, made a straight refusal while Bhagat Singh suggested the name of Lala Dunichand, which the Tribunal readily accepted.

Rajguru had been successful in obstructing the proceedings with his linguistic drama in Magistrate's Court. Though Tribunal provided him with on interpreter right from the first day, but Noad was not to give up so easily. He managed to produce many witnesses, testifying to Rajguru's multilingual capabilities.

Mukund Pant Shastri, a teacher in Sangved Sanskrit Vidhyalaya, Kashi (PW 11) deposed that during Rajguru's stay with him at Kashi for two and a half years as a student, he observed him as understanding and speaking the *Dakkhini* or Marathi language. He never heard him speaking in either Hindi or Urdu, therefore, he is not certain about Rajguru's linguistic skills.

Syed Ahmed Shah, D.S.P., C.I.D., Lahore (PW 411). who escorted Rajguru from Pune to Lahore, testified that during the journey, Rajguru had conversed with him in Hindi as well as in English. E. Mills, Inspector, City Kotwali, Pune (PW 413) stated that Rajguru had been talking to Dinkar, his brother in mostly English and partly Marathi. He could speak English fluently. Khwaja Tejuddin, Inspector, Lahore (PW 9), who had been a part of the escort team from Pune to Lahore, also confirmed that Rajguru had talked to him in English as well as in Hindi at the time of arrest and during transit and he felt that Rajguru could understand English reasonably well.

Bakhshi Deenanath, Inspector (PW 8) deposed that he had many talks with Rajguru during investigations in Lahore Fort and during intervals in the Court and observed that he could understand and speak Urdu and had a reasonable understanding of English too. Justice Agha Hyder asked the witness whether the Public Prosecutor had stated before the Tribunal on first day that Rajguru understands English as well as Hindi language. Noad immediately objected to the process of questioning by the Court. Justice Agha Hyder made a mention of this in the proceedings, treating this as an obstruction. Hansraj, Assistant Jailor, Borstal Institute, Lahore (PW 10) testified that he had talks with Rajguru during his stay in the Jail. Rajguru and colleagues shared the same barrack and conversed freely with each other in English, Hindi and Urdu languages.

Here it would be worth mentioning that he was denied participation in Assembly Bomb Case by Azad on the ground that he could not comprehend English well. All testimony serves to prove that he was proficient in Hindi, Sanskrit, Marathi and Urdu. His knowledge of English was limited but he had developed his English too in company of his colleagues, especially Bhagat Singh, before and during his stay in the Jail.

The services of the interpreter, provided by the Tribunal on 5th May 1930, had been terminated on 14th May, due to boycott of the Court by the accused. When Rai Bahadur J.N. Banerjee, D.S.P., C.I.E. (PW 26) and J. Path, A.S.I., Champaran (Bihar) were examined on 26th June, 1930, Rajguru himself, like a professional advocate, had cross-examined him using all his logic and argumentative skills.

Jitendra Nath Sanyal made a historical opening speech before the Tribunal and cast severe aspersions on the Government. He said, "The British have killed so many innocent Indians, which can not be avenged. To enslave somebody is the greatest crime against the mankind and British are guilty of it. They intend to suppress the independence, the most fundamental right of the people, by using power. We, revolutionaries, are not the accused before the law, but the saviours of the national pride and self-respect. In reality, the persons representing this tyrannical government are real culprits." Justice Coldstream. immediately, restrained his statement from the proceedings, on the grounds of this being unrelated and promoting treason.

The statement, though, had served its purpose. The unrest in the Court had already erupted with shouting of the slogans *'Inquilaab Zindabad'* 'Down with the imperialism'. Sanyal continued. "This trial is only a charade. We refuse to be a part of it and dissociate ourselves."

The episode turned Justice Coldstream into a far more biased person, whose only aim now was to bring revolutionaries on their knees. The slogan raising served to infuriate him further.

On 12th May, the proceedings started dot on time. The accused started raising slogans and singing partiotic songs, despite strict orders by the President. They started singing these famous lines from the great poet. Omprakash:

Apni kismet mein azal se hi sitam rakkha tha,
Ranj rakkha tha, Muhim Rakkhi thi, Gam Rakkha tha;

Kisko parwah thi aur kisme dum rakkha tha,
Humne jab vaadi-e-gurbat mein kadam rakkha tha;
Dur tak yaad-e-watan aai thi samjhane ko.

Justice Coldstream ordered the Police to restrain the accused. As it had happened earlier, the Police started merciless, cruel assault on the helpless revolutionaries with shoes and canes. Then their hands and feet were tied.

The proceedings were put to halt. Justice Coldstream and Justice Hilton mentioned in the proceeding book that the case was adjourned till tomorrow, owing to the disorderly conduct of the accused and the Court was cleared with the removal of the accused. But justice Agha Hyder, disagreeing with his fellow judges. remarked. "I was not a party to the order of removal of the accused from the Court to the Jail and I was not responsible for it anyway. I dissociate myself from all that took place here today."

This incident served to benefits the revolutionaries as now everyone agreed to boycott the proceedings. All the accused refused to attend the court from 13th May 1930 and threatened to continue doing so unless the President of the Tribunal offered an unqualified apology for these orders. The trial, which had run a smooth course for about a week now turned into a one sided battle, which the accused knew they were certain to lose. The proceedings, however, continued despite the absence of the accused.

Justice Coldstream communicated to the Viceroy, through Governor of Punjab, that it was impossible to award death sentence to Bhagat Singh and other accused, as long as Justice Agha Hyder was a member of the Tribunal.

three and a quarter month, merely completing the formalities. It is noteworthy that Tribunal used to record the statements only on Mondays, Tuesdays and Wednesdays every week.

The Tribunal, in absence of accused, also framed the charges against them. According to the order, Master Agyaram, Surendra Nath Pandey and Batukeshwar Dutt were discharged due to lack of evidence. In reality, the prosecution had retracted the case against Dutt, as he was already serving life sentence in Assembly Bomb Case. The Fifteen accused, including Bhagat Singh, Sukhdev, Rajguru, Kishorilal, Deshraj, Prem Dutt, Jaidev Kapoor, Shiv Verma, Gaya Prasad, Mahaveer Singh. Ajay Kumar Ghosh, Jitendra Kumar Sanyal, Vijay Kumar Sinha, Kundanlal and K.N. Tiwari were to face charges of possessing arms, ammunition and explosive substances, commiting and attempting to commit murder, robbery and dacoity, rescuing and attempting to rescue persons detained in lawful custody and waging and attempting to wage war against the King under Section 121, 121-A, 122, 123, 302 read with 120-B, 109, 114,115 and 116 of the Indian Penal Code and Sections 4-A, 4-B, 5 and 6 of the Explosive Substances Act, 1908.

As none of the accused were present in the Court, the Tribunal issued the orders to deliver a copy of the charges to each of the accused in Jail. Malik Fateh Khan, the Registrar, informed the Tribunal on the next day that one copy of the translated version of the charges was sent to Rajguru through B.W. Thate, but he declined to acknowledge it.

As none of the accused appeared or made a statement on the charges made against him, the

Tribunal, under Section 256 of the Criminal Procedure Code and Section 9 (2) of the Ordinance inferred that they were deemed to have pleaded not-guilty.

Azad planned to rescue Bhagat Singh and colleagues on 1st June 1930 but the attempt was foiled. The revolutionaries had established their headquartes at Bahawalpur Road midway between the Jail and the Poonchh House. They had planned to disrupt the police cordon by throwing a bomb by Vaishampayan and carry out the rescue operation during chaos.

Bhagat Singh thought otherwise as he was deeply aggrieved by sad demise of Bhagwati Charan, his college time friend. He did not want to escape; rather he was quite eager to embrace death for the supreme cause. He, therefore, did not reply to flute sound signal from Vaishampayan. This saddened Azad further.

The Verdict

The Lahore Conspiracy Case may be one of the most significant cases in the Indian scene from the historical perspective, but one of the worst cases from the judicial point of view. The detail study of the proceeding book suggests that the court was against the accused right from the beginning and remained biased till the very end. The Court did not pay any regard to the fundamental principles of the natural justice under the false cover of the special powers given by the Ordinance to suppress the voice of the freedom fighters.

The prosecution based its case on the story concocted by the approvers, Fanindra Nath, Jai Gopal and Hansraj Vohra. They were the star witnesses for the Government as, being colleagues of Bhagat Singh and other revolutionaries, they had complete knowledge as to what had transpired at Mozang House Road. Fanindra Nath Ghosh, being a member of the Central Committee himself, had the first hand knowledge of the organization and activities of Hindustan Socialist Republican Army. Jai Gopal was an eye witness as well as integral part of the conspiracy to assassinate Saunders while Vohra was well apprised of activities of Bhagat Singh and his colleagues.

The prosecution had recorded the detailed statements of all three approvers on priority, even before framing of the charges. The statement of Jai Gopal (PW 2), recorded from 3rd to 16th may 1930, appears on pages 9 to 59 of the proceeding book. The statement of Fanindra Nath Ghosh (PW 3), recorded from 16th to 28th May 1930, appears on pages 67 to 141 of the proceeding book while the statement of Hans Raj Vohra (PW 5), recorded from 28th to 30th May 1930, appears on pages 165 to 193 of the proceeding book. It was quite lengthy considering that these witnesses were not cross-examined; otherwise this would have taken double the time.

None of the accused ever appeared in the court after the framing of the charges. The Tribunal, taking one sided action, mechanically recorded the statements of 432 prosection witnesses within a short period of one and a half months, without cross-examination or any other participation by the accused. The court proceedings had been converted into merely a high profile drama.

The Traffic Inspector Ferns (PW 46) was the most important witness for the prosecution as he had seen Bhagat Singh and Rajguru firing on Saunders and chased both in pursuit. Astonishingly, he failed to identify both in the jail as well as Court. Gendalal, Habibullah and his nephew, Noor Mohammed testified to seeing and identifying both of them at the site of incident. The Tribunal relied upon their testimony, but without showing any reasonable basis.

Lt. Col. J.G.G. Swan, Civil Surgeon, Lahore (PW 133), the surgeon who had performed autopsy on the body of Saunders, was an important witness from Rajguru's perspective. He testified to the post-mortem report and stated that the injury no. O-3 was half an inch sized gun shot entry wound located on left side of the chest, accompanied by the fracture of the fifth rib.

This was the only bullet fired by Rajguru, which proved fatal. Dr. A.E. Matthews (PW 118) testified to the post-mortem report of Head Constable Channan Singh, who was fired upon by Azad.

The prosecution presented Ram Prasad (PW 58), Hussain Bakhsh (PW 64, Buddhu (PW 73), Gaman (PW 74), Fakir Chand (PW 86), Mirza Abdul Aziz Baig (PW 239) and Ram Dulare (PW 238) who gave their testimony before the tribunal about seeing and identifying Rajguru on the date of killing, his presence in Lahore and at Mozang House separately.

In the meantime, Bhagat Singh and all other accused, barring Prem Dutt and Kundanlal, began their third round of hunger strike on 28th July 1930 against inhuman treatment given to the accused in jail and unlawful attitude of the Tribunal. Batukeshwar, meanwhile Multan Jail, joined them in the strike.

Rajguru lost 19 pounds of weight this time and developed insomnia. Godavari, his sister and Seetabai, the sister-in-law visited him. The sister raised the possibility of life imprisonment. Then Rajguru said, "Death would be far better than rotting behind the bars for years. Do not mourn if I am hanged. I will be born again to accomplish the unfinished task."

Tribunal had examined 457 witnesses by 26th August 1930. On this date the public prosecutor gave up remaining 256 witnesses and closed the case for the prosecution. The Tribunal, on 26th passed an order adjourning the case for next day to question the accused generally on the case, in accordance with the Section 343 of the Criminal Procedure Code, before putting up their defense. The copies of the order were served to all accused inside the jail.

Next day, the Tribunal dispensed with the attendance of all accused, as they resisted being produced in the Court. The Tribunal passed another order, requiring the accused to put up their defense, along with the evidence. The copy of this order was served to all accused.

None of the accused appeared before the tribunal on 28th and 29th August 1930. The Tribunal, as usual, recorded the formal statements of Bakhshilal, Assistant Jailor, Borstal Institute, Doulat Ali Shah, Assistant Jailor and Major M. Fazaldeen, Superintendent, Central Jail, Lahore, who testified on personally giving the order to the accused and their subsequent refusal to attend the Court. No defense witness appeared on their behalf nor did they submit any list of defense witnesses to be summoned. The Tribunal continued to act under Section 9 of the Ordinance but, just to project Government's image as being judicious and impartial, the proceedings were adjourned.

On 1st September 1930, the accused again resisted appearance in the Court and their presence was once again dispensed with. However, they ended their hunger strike, as Justice Hilton passed an order regarding provision of all facilities to them inside the jail. On the same day, Mr. Amolak Ram Kapoor made an application on behalf of Vijay Kumar Sinha and Ajay Ghosh, for the recall of cross-examination of all 457 prosecution witnesses in the interest of the justice as their testimony, particularly approvers' was recorded without prior notice to the accused. He also requested for one week adjournment as he required time to study the copies of the statements and the proceeding book received only the previous evening. The Tribunal, regarded this petition as baseless and dilatory, refused to entertain it and thus ended all chances of defence for the accused.

The same day, the Public Prosecutor commenced his arguments, which were over by 10th September. The accused were ordered to be produced next day to put up any arguments. They did not turn up and the case was adjourned till 8th October for judgment. The fate was sealed.

Sardar Kishan Singh, father of Bhagat Singh, submitted a petition before the Tribunal on 20th September 1930 and pleaded that on the date of Saunder's assassination, Bhagat Singh was in Calcutta and from there, he posted a letter to Ramlal, Manager, Khadi Department, Pari Mahal Lahore, which had reached Lahore by post. To prove this alibi, Bhagat Singh should be given a chance for defense by bringing Ramlal in the dock.

Bhagat Singh, on learning this, openly resented this move by writing a letter, which was published in the 'Tribune'. He wrote, "You have no right to make an application on my behalf, without consulting me. I fail to understand your weakness at this crucial juncture, while you have devoted yourself to the cause of our nation." The Tribunal dismissed the petition on the ground that Bhagat Singh, himself, was not interested in any consideration on the application.

The hearing of the case had already been over by September 1930. The Tribunal was to last till 17th October 1930, therefore, the judgment had to be delivered before that date. It was being awaited with great interest but no specific date for deliverance had been declared by the Tribunal, considering the great public unrest and the deteriorating law and order situation.

Khan Bahadur Mohammed Akbar Khan, the Jail Superintendent and an ardent Government servant, had developed great regard and affection, for these great youth. He arranged a farewell dinner in their respect inside the jail on 5th October 1930, which was attended by many jail officials too. Some curious wives of British officers too attended, just to have a glimpse of the heroes. They were all amazed to see these vibrant and cheerful youth, enjoying every moment of the celebration, even in the face of imminent death. That night, they moved closest to every heart further in those lighter moments as they were not brutal revolutionaries alone but were also filled with zeal and respect for life.

October 7th, 1930

The fateful day had arrived. The security had been put on highest alert. The registrar of the Lahore High Court, as a special envoy of the Tribunal, came to the Jail, along with 281 page decision. He called each of them one by one and delivered the historical decision.

Master Agyaram, Desraj, Ajay Ghosh and Surendra Nath pandey were acquitted for want of evidence. Other accused were sentenced as follows:

Death Sentence

1. Bhagat Singh
2. Shivram Rajguru
3. Sukhdev

Life Imprisonment

1. Vijay K. Sinha
2. Mahaveer Singh
3. Kishorilal
4. Jaidev Kapoor
5. Gaya Prasad
6. Shiv Verma

7. Kamal Nath Tiwari

Imprisonment

1. Kundanlal (7 years)
2. Prem Dutt (5 years)

The awardees of death sentence were given free copies of the decision. They expressed great joy on the pronouncement of the judgment and embraced each other warmly. Their glowing faces amazed their colleagues as well as the officials and loud shouts of "Inquilaab Zindabad" and "Long Live India" emerged almost at once.

Rajguru's mother, Parvati Devi, accompanied by Yamutai Bhatwadekar, also happened to visit the Jail on the same day. They were not aware of the day of deliverance of the judgment. They had come with *shrikhand*, *matar usal* and *peda*, which Bhagat Singh and Batukeshwar Dutt relished most. She was excited at the enthusiasm of her children for the dishes of their choice. The warders checked the food as a way of routine and informed, in subdued tone, about the judgment. Learning the news of award of death sentence to Bhagat Singh, Sukhdev and Rajguru, the mother's whole world was shattered and she was immediately at the loss of words.

Yamutai, unable to suppress her feelings, started crying. She was in a dilemma as to how to face the children and offer them the sweets, when the news for their death sentence had just been broken. She contemplated going back but the mother had different thoughts. Rajguru's words: "Mother, you have two sons, just take it that one belongs to you and another to Mother India" kept ringing in her ears repeatedly. It dawned upon her that this was not the moment to shed tears over the martyrs, rather to greet them. With a new determination, she, along with Yamutai, started walking towards the barrack of her gallant sons to offer them her blessings.

Rajguru and his colleagues were elated at the sight of mother and immediately gathered around her, curious about the food. They at once started devouring the dishes. The mother remained calm but Yamutai was shaky. While removing the packet of *Lahori peda*, she could not contain herself and started crying aloud. The atmosphere suddenly turned grim and the silence was broken only by her sounds of crying. The brave mother, somehow maintaining her composure, gently caressed Yamutai and said, "What a coincidence! We never expected to hear the bad news today. Just have a look at my face and calm down."

Mother Parvati indeed was courage personified. She had encountered turbulent times on many occasions during her long life. She had already suffered the misfortunes of being widowed at early age and her younger son leaving the house at a very tender age. Despite being without support from her elder son, Dinkar, she, retained her courage and self-confidence and kept shuttling between Pune and Lahore. Bhagat Singh's Mother Vihyawati had rightly said these prophetic words. "If God could make some fine arrangements for transference of the troubles of the children to their mother, then no mother would have allowed her son to remain sad even for a moment."

Rajguru, too, caressed Yamutai to console her. Cheerfully, they started to devour the dishes again mother, gazing at those vibrant youth continuously and wondered that these were the last moments of happiness for them before death.

The time for meeting got over. On her way back, the mother wilted under the pressure and started crying. She turned breathless due to crying and asthma.

She was unaware that the wide open eyes of her now helpless son, too, were following her. The mother's grief had pierced his hard shell too. He had already started remembering the golden moments spent with his ever-caring mother and other beloved ones, appearing like a movie on the screen. The joy of receiving the death sentence as desired rewards for the love of the nation was getting replaced by the sorrow of observing his sick, weakened, elderly mother walking back alone, wiping her tears. He felt depressed by the thought that her already bad health would be seriously jolted by the news of his death.

The 281 page judgment, delivered by three member Tribunal, had details about the evidence against each of the accused. The judgment also included the inferences made by the Tribunal after evaluating the evidence, in relation to Rajguru's role in Lahore Conspiracy Case. The verbatim citation of the opinion about Rajguru made by the learned Judges is as follows:

Shivram Rajguru

This accused, who is also known by the alias 'M' is a *Marhatta* and was arrested at Pune on the 30th September 1929, by inspector Mills (PW 413) and Syed Ahmed Shah, Deputy Superintedent of Police (PW 411)

Shivram Rajguru was not present at the Delhi meeting of September 1928, and his first appearance on the scene was his arrival in Lahore on the 17th November 1928, when he came with Kundanlal from Ferozepur and was met by Jai Gopal at the Railway Station and taken to the Mozang House. Shivram Rajguru was a gun man and he was evidently brought to Lahore to take part in the raid on the Punjab National Bank, Lahore and in the murder of Mr. Scott, which required a man skilled in the use of arms. He took part in the Punjab National Bank affair and was one of the murderers of Mr. Saunders. He was also present in the meetings held at the Mozang House at which these affairs were discussed.

He left with Bhagat Singh on 20th December, travelling as Bhagat Singh's servant.

The evidence of Shivram Rajguru's presence in Lahore is that of Jai Gopal and Hans Raj Vohra, approvers, corroborated by the statement of Ram Parshad (PW 58), who identified him at a magisterial parade and also the Court as having frequented the house of Mussamat Parbati in Gowalmandi; the confession of Mahabir Singh who met Shivram Rajguru at the Mozang House and knew him at that time by the name of Raghu Nath; and the evidence of Hussain Baksh (PW 64), Buddhu (PW 73), Gaman (PW 74) and Fakir Chand (PW 86), all of whom identified Shivram Rajguru at magisterial parades as well as in Court as a man who frequented the Mozang House. The evidence of Jai Gopal and the confession of Mahabir Singh are particularly important in proving the guilt of Shivram Rajguru in all matters in which they mention him. Mahabir Singh's confession gives a description of the man whom he knew as Raghu Nath and this tallies with the appearance of Shivram Rajguru.

The proof that Shivram Rajguru participated in the Punjab National Bank affair is the evidence of Jai Gopal and Hans Raj Vohra corroborated by the confession of Mahabir Singh and this participation is fully proved.

Shivram Rajguru is proved to have been one of the murderers of Mr. Saunders by the evidence of Jai Gopal who also took part in that affair, corroborated by numerous other pieces of evidence. In the first place, there is confession of Mahabir Singh that at the meeting where the murder of Mr. Scott was discussed, it was resolved that Raghu Nath alias Shivram Rajguru should be one of the murderers and further that Shivram Rajguru was present at the Mozang House on the meeting of the 17th December 1928 with Panditji, Bhagat Singh, Jai Gopal and others and that at about 4 or 5 p.m. Bhagat Singh, Panditji and Raghu Nath returned to the Mozang House together on bicycles. Next, there is evidence of some of the eye witnesses of the murder and of the retreat of the murderers after the murder which has been mentioned above, in discussing the case against Bhagat Singh. Of those eye witnesses, the majority described the two murderers as being the tallish man and a shorter man and this description fits the two men, Bhagat Singh and Shivram Rajguru respectively.

Abdullah (PW 34), the driver of the taxi, which drew up while the murder was going satisfactorily, identified Shivram Rajguru, both at the magisterial parade and also in Court as one of the two men who actually fired upon Mr. Saunders. The remaining eye witnesses of the actual murder are disregarded for the reasons already stated in connection with the case against Bhagat Singh. But Mr. Feam (PW 46), though he did not identify anybody, gave a description in the report Ex. P.A.T. which he drew up immediately after the murder, of one of the two men, who had fired the shots and whom he stated to be 5'5" in height and to have a thin moustache, which description might apply to Shivram Rajguru. Ajmer Singh (PW 181) is the student from whom the three murderers tried to take a bicycle and he has identified Shivram Rajguru at the magisterial parade and also in Court as one of those three men, though it should be added that at the magesterial parade, his identification was not very definite, what he said being that Shivram Rajguru was possibly one of those men but that he could not be sure as the man whom he had in his mind had been a little stronger than Shivram Rajguru appeared to be at the time of the parade. This parade was held on the 7th October 1929, nearly 10 months after the murder (see the evidence of Ch. Mushtaq Ahmed (PW 33). The other witnessess who saw the retreat of the murderer, such as Som Nath (PW 144) and Abnash Chand (PW 145), testified that they were three in number and no suggestion has been made at any time that any person other then Shivram Rajguru was the third one of the three. Having regard to the consideration above mentioned, the statement of Jai Gopal and Mahabir Singh made long before Shivram Rajguru was arrested, and having regard to the evidence of Abdullah (PW 34) and Ajmer Singh (PW 181), it is fully proved that Shivram Rajguru was one of the two men who fired upon Mr. Saunders.

Regarding the departure of Shivram Rajguru with Bhagat Singh from Lahore on the 20th December 1928, there is little evidence of Jai Gopal and Hans Raj Vohra, corroborated by that of the four railway officials who have already been mentioned while discussing Bhagat Singh's case namely Ram Saran Dass (PW 114), Hari Chand (PW 115), Niaz-ud-din (PW 116) and Tej Singh (PW 117). Whether Shivram Rajguru was present at Agra and was a member of the rescue party of Jogesh Chander Chatterjee, is proved by the evidence of Fanindra Nath Ghosh, who also knew Shivram Rajguru by the name of Raghunath and is corroborated as well by the evidence of Lalit Kumar Mukerjee from Allahabad to Agra to assist in the making of bombs. Lalit Kumar Mukerjee identified Shivram Rajguru at a magisterial parade. There is corrobration of this evidence in the statement of Beni Parshad (PW 236), who identified Shivram Rajguru at a magisterial parade as one of the men who had rented the Noori Gate at Agra and at the time of that identification, this witness pointed at Shivram Rajguru though he subsequently failed to identify him in Court; also in the statement of Abdul Aziz Beg (PW 239) who identified Shivram Rajguru both at a magisterial parade and also in Court as having frequented the Hing ki Mandi house. Regarding his participation in the rescue party of Jogesh Chander Chatterjee, here is evidence of two railway officials, Ramlal (PW 270) and Din Dayal (PW 271), which corroborate the statement of Fanindra Nath Ghosh that seven persons travelled on that occasion from Agra to Kanpur. In view of this evidence, Shivram Rajguru's association with other members of the party at Agra is sufficiently proved.

The evidence regarding Shivram Rajguru's presence at Ferozepur is not satisfactory and does not amount to proof, the witness on the point being Gajju Ram (PW 295) and Ram Saran Dass (PW 308), neither of whom identified Shivram Rajguru in a satisfactory manner.

Fanindra Nath Ghosh mentions that Shivram Rajguru went from Agra to Delhi as men were required at Delhi for the action and the presence of Shivram Rajguru at Delhi prior to the Assembly Bomb affair receives confirmation from the evidence of Nur Muhammad (PW 174), who identified him both in Court and a magisterial parade as having frequented the house of Ram Saran Dass at Delhi. The visit to Delhi is proved by this evidence.

When he was arrested at Pune on the 30th September 1999, a revolver and 14 cartridges were found lying in a tin box near where Shivram Rajguru was sleeping (see the evidence of Inspector Mills (PW 413) and Said Ahmed Shah, Deputy Superintedent of Police (PW 411), a fact which is relevant to prove his character as a gun man. The truth of the evidence of Dattatreya Balwant Karandikar (PW 416) is doubtful and is, therefore, disregarded.

To sum up against Shivram Rajguru alias 'M', he was brought to Lahore in November 1928 to take part in the raid on the Punjab National Bank and he actually took part in the Bank robbery and was also one of the two men, who fired upon Mr. Saunders. He is proved to have visited the house which the members of the party used at Jhansi and he was also at Agra in February 1929 and was a member of the rescue party of Jogesh Chandar Chatterjee. From Agra, he went to Delhi before the bomb was thrown in the Assembly Hall. When arrested at Pune in September 1929, a revolver and cartidges were found near him.

In the last paragraph of the judgment, the Tribunal declared as follows : 'Shivram Rajguru alias 'M' is convicted under Sections 121 and 302 of the Indian Penal Code. In view of his participation in the murder of Mr. Saunders, he is sentenced to be hanged by neck till he is dead".

Though the government had taken all possible measures to contain the information, but the news about the sentence, within moments, spread like wildfire throughout Lahore, and the whole of the country. The local administration, in anticipation, had immediately enforced Section 144, banning any gathering or procession, but a huge crowd gathered at the Municipal

Ground on 7th October itself, without any prior intimation or preparation. The gathering openly condemned the unlawful Ordinance, one sided trial and the death sentences. Many prominent dailies brought out special editions, highlighting Bhagat Singh, Rajguru and Sukhdev.

Next day, on 8th October, people of Lahore, mostly youth, came out in the open more strongly. The whole city observed strike on the call of Students' Union. All the educational institutes were closed. Hundreds of students, including 17 females, were arrested. Professor Janak Kumari Zutshi, a Professor in the Girl's College, Lahore resigned from her post and was arrested along with her mother and sisters. 90 D.A.V. College students, led by a Professor, gheraoed the Police. The Police resorted to lathi charge, culminating in the death of the teacher.

Unarmed people were subjected to heavy assault by the police, when attempting to get the Government College closed, where the children of the British studied. Noujawan Bharat Sabha organized a huge protest demonstration at Bradlaugh Hall, where partiotic slogans were raised. Congress also organized a heavy rally at Mori Gate, which was led by Parvati Devi, daughter of Lala Lajpat Rai. The whole city continued to echo with the slogans, 'Long Live Bhagat Singh', 'Long live Rajguru' and 'Long Live Sukhdev' throughout the day.

On 9th October, Parvatibai, Rajguru's mother, was denied a meeting with her son, despite waiting at the gates till 5.30 in the evening. This news was published in 'The Tribune', next day.

The scenario was no different in other cities of the country. Amritsar and rest of Punjab presented a picture similar to that at Lahore. There was severe public unrest, being exhibited in the form of strike, dharna, protest demonstration and rallies, at Calcutta, Bombay, Nagpur, Madras, Delhi, Patna, Lucknow, Kanpur, Benaras, Allahabad and all other places.

The whole nation was shocked to its core and felt hurt and insulted at this judgment. The empathetic voices of the millions of the suppresed Indians echoed together, seeking their release. There erupted violent reactions when a sleeping nation was suddenly aroused by this event. When the news crossed the boundaries of the nation, many foreign governments also condemned the unlawful procedure adopted by British and called for either condoning of sentence or release of the revolutionaries.

According to the warrant issued by the Tribunal, the hanging was scheduled on 27th October 1930, but this date was postponed. The final difference of 167 days between the pronouncement of the judgment and execution was quite a long one, and during this period, Lahore served as the trigger point for the heavy protests and strikes throughout the nation.

The defence committee started intensive campaigning under the leadership of Sardar Kishan Singh, Bhagat Singh's father. Similar 'Bhagat Singh Appeal Committees' were formed in various cities of Punjab with a sole aim to move the public to participate in anti-government demonstrations. At Lahore and Amritsar, million of people affixed their signature on the memorandum addressed to the Viceroy seeking commutation of death sentence to life imprisonment. Bhagat Singh, Sukhdev and Rajguru had, indeed, achieved the status of super heroes in the minds of the public, far surpassing any contemporary political leader.

The countdown

The defence committee was very keen to move the Privy Council against the Tribunal's order in Lahore Conspiracy Case, though the Ordinance categorically specified that the decision made by the Tribunal was final and no appeal could be made against such order. The only way out possible was a petition challenging the legality of the constitution of the Tribunal as the accused had neither appeared in the Court nor cross-examined any of the prosecution witnesses. The revolutionaries feared that in event of Privy Council Judges remaining impartial, and on account of technical flaws, they could pass an order for commuting the death sentence, or even cancel the Tribunal's orders. They did not want anything to happen which could come in the way of their supreme sacrifice.

Pandit Motilal Nehru, a true friend of the revolutionaries, despite being on death bed, sent a message from Shimla that to keep the possibility of the commutation of the death sentence, the appeal must be filed before the Privy Council. Bhagat Singh and his colleagues, after serious contemplation, reached at a conclusion that the appeal would also serve to popularize their ideology of freedom struggle and the real stories of atrocities inflicted by British over the political prisoners and Indian public in general, at the international level. The sympathy generated would thus boost the morale of

Rajguru's Room in D.A.V. Collage Kanpur

Box of Rajguru

Hanuman Prasarak Mandal, Amravati

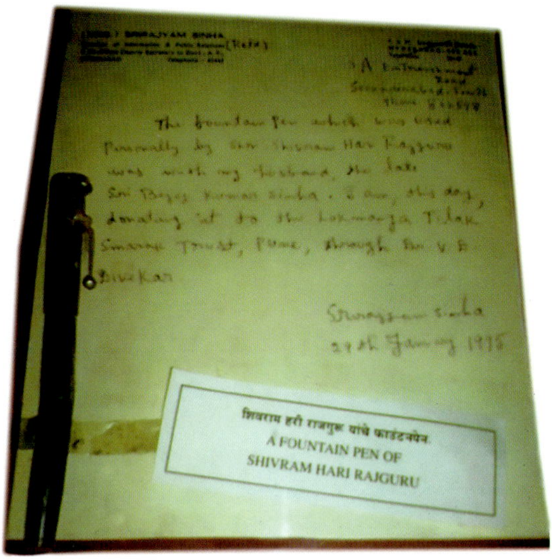

Fountain Pen of Rajguru

Hutatma Shivram Hari Rajguru Memorial

Samadhi of three ravolutionaries in Hussainiwala

Rajguru's statue in Rajguru Nagar

millions of Indians and thus the move was deemed as politically advantageous.

The petition was presented before the Privy Council in November 1930. It primarily challenged the legality of the Ordinance of 1930, promulgated by Viceroy and Governor-General of India, which led to the constitution of the Tribunal. The petition was heard on 11th February 1931 by five Judges of the Privy Council, namely Justice Wycount Dunedin, Lord Thackerson, Lord Rousell, Sir George Lawdess and Sir Dinshaw Mullah at Council Chamber, White Hall, London. D.N. Pritt, representing the accused, argued over the Petition of Special Leave to appeal and challenged the legality of the Ordinance and Tribunal.

The Appeal was turned down, as expected, on the grounds that Governor General had the authority to promulgate the impugned Ordinance and that was done in accordance with law. The study of the certified copy of the arguments, procured by me from National Archives, New Delhi, clearly indicates that the Duke of Wellington was definitely biased against the accused. This case has been cited as Bhagat Singh and Anr. Vs. The King Emperor, 1931, Indian Law Reports Lahore Series, Page 280.

The legal battle did not stop here. Chintaram Thapar, uncle of Sukhdev, filed another petition before the Lahore High Court on the ground that the death sentence of Bhagat Singh, Sukhdev and Rajguru was fixed on 27th October 1930. The Tribunal, which had passed the order, has ceased to exist. Now under what authority, they can be hanged or being detained in the custody.

Prominent lawyers. Bhagat Ram Puri and Amolak Ram represented the petitioner before the Court while the Government was represented by C.H. Conrod Noad, the public prosecutor before the Tribunal too. The High Court summarily dismissed the petition on 25th February 1931 on the ground that since the impugned order by the Tribunal had already been challenged before the Privy Council, therefore, the Local Government had all powers, under Section 401 of the Criminal Procedure Code, to commute or reinstate the order of the death sentence. No fresh warrant, therefore, was needed to be issued for the execution of death sentence. Similarly, the solitary detention of such prisoners was also not unlawful. The Court also opined that the Local Government, under Section 402 of the Criminal Procedure Code, had the powers, if deemed proper in event of some legal technical problem, to commute death sentence to exile or life imprisonment. This case has been cited as Chintaram Thapar Vs. The King Emperor, A.I.R. 1931, Lahore, Page 359.

On 19th February 1931, mother Vidyawati, out of emotions to save her son, filed a mercy petition before the Viceroy. Sardar Kishan Singh had already made a similar effort previously. Bhagat Singh was deeply annoyed with his parents for such efforts. He could never dream of pleading amnesty before such tyrannical rule. He and his colleagues were, however, happy to sacrifice themselves for their nation.

The whole country was rife with protests, demonstrations and dharnas. The patriotic slogans were raised everywhere. Their colleagues planned to rescue them, but Bhagwaticharan's unfortunate death shattered the organization and thus all plans to seek their release.

The trio had become so popular that every Indian identified himself with them and never wanted to part with them. Every youth's heart was filled with the desire to follow the ideal "Life for life". They sung the following lines:

Bhagat Singh ke khoon ka asar dekh lena,
Mita denge jalim ka ghar dekh lena.

(Observe the effect of Bhagat Singh's martyrdom; we will demolish the tyrant's home (Government).

Azad, too much eager to have his colleagues released, moved to Allahabad to negotiate with some political leaders. Some traitor leaked the news to police. The police stormed the Alfred Park (now called Azad Park) and engaged in heavy gun firing with Azad. His colleague ran away, but Azad, sensing that escape was impossible, shot himself with his Mouser. He had always maintained that he can never be apprehended alive and his death proved him right. The dusk over the Indian revolution scene had already set in.

With the passage of time, the despair increased further. The Viceroy House was flooded with memoranda and telegrams signed by thousands of Indians. The King of Bikaner and other Indian rulers, too, forwarded their mercy appeals.

On 14th February, eminent leader Pandit Madan Mohan Malviya sent a telegram to the Viceroy to request him to use his prerogative of mercy in cases of Bhagat Singh, Rajguru and Sukhdev and commute their death sentences to life imprisonment. Some members of the Lower House of British Parliament also wrote to Viceroy that the Free Labour Party of the House of Commons, keeping in view the agreement, openly request you to commute the sentences of Lahore Conspiracy Case accused. The Viceroy received the telegram of 6th March 1931. The British Communist too remarked that this trial is a true representative of use of inhuman and barbaric treatment for political victimisation.

Gandhiji and other prominent leaders were released on 25th January 1931. The Congress and the Government soon entered into negotiations. The Congress Working Committee vested all its authority in the hands of Mahatma Gandhi. This aroused hopes of survival for these revolutionaries among the public, as a favourable deal could now be struck. This was not to happen. The gloom deepened further by the absence of provision of commutation for the accused in Gandhi-Irwin Pact, executed on 4th February 1931.

On 17th February, Bhagat Ram Puri, Kabeeruddin Ahmed and Gaya Prasad Singh raised the question of commutation of the sentence in the Central Assembly at Delhi. James Cramer, the Treasury member, could offer no satisfactory answer. He referred to Sir George Rainey, who, on 5th February, declared that the Government would not make any compromises with the accused on the path of armed revolution.

On 17th March, Netaji Subhas Chandra Bose, while addressing a large gathering at Azad Maidan, Delhi, also called upon to commute the death sentences. But all efforts were futile.

On 18th March 1931, Prannath Mehta, a close friend and counsel of Bhagat Singh, put forward a suggestion before Bhagat Singh, Sukhdev and Rajguru that now their life had become a national treasure and they would be required to shape the independent India. Therefore, as a last resort, they should file a mercy petition themselves for the commutation.

All three turned serious. Sukhdev and Rajguru appeared, little tense, but Bhagat Singh calmly asked, "What type of appeal you wish us to make." Rajguru was enraged, but Bhagat Singh's influence kept him under check.

Prannath Mehta felt a little embarrassed. “Do not get me wrong, friends. We will never talk a thing which will downgrade your bravery. We will prepare the draft tonight in the meeting and I will bring it to you tomorrow morning.”

Next morning, Mehta returned with the draft. Bhagat Singh greeted him with a smile and said, “Now we do not need the draft. We have already sent the petition as the time was really short. Please go through this too.”

Mehta was in great shock after reading it. The petition was written in a very lively and moving manner and signed by them. Most significantly, this is the only document during history of Lahore Conspiracy Case, which bears Rajguru’s signature. Few important excerpts are as follows:

“That the main charge against us was that of having waged war against H.M. King George, the King of England. The above mentioned finding of the Court presupposed two things: Firstly, that there exists a state of war between the British nation and the Indian nation and, secondly, that we had actually participated in that war and were therefore war prisoners. The second presupposition seems to be a little bit flattering, but nevertheless it is too tempting to resist the desire of acquiescence in it.”

“As to the question of our fates, please allow us to say that when you have decided to put us to death, you will certainly do it. You have got the power in your hands and the power is the greatest justification in this world. We know that the maxim ‘Might is right’ serves as your guiding motto. The whole of our trial was just a proof of that. We wanted to point out that according to the verdict of your court, we had waged war and were therefore war prisoners. And we claim to be treated as such, i.e., we claim to be shot dead instead of to be hanged. It rests with you to prove that you really meant what your court has said. We request and hope that you will very kindly order the military department to send its detachment to perform our execution."

Yours'

Bhagat Singh, Rajguru and Sukhdev

This letter, written only three days prior to their hanging, is itself representative of the boldness and self-pride of these great martyrs.

History also tells us that Lord Irwin, under immense public pressure, had almost decided to commute the death sentences, but all British officers of the Punjab cadre threatended to resign en masse in event of his doing so. This news had appeared in the newspaper *Bhavishya* on 2nd April 1931. They were always scared of these three youth when they were free and remained so even after their imprisonment.

Bhagat Sigh, Rajguru and Sukhdev had to be transferred to separate cells, as per provision of solitary detention for death sentence convicts according to Jail Manual. They embraced each other warmly and started their journey to their respective barracks.

Rajguru had become far naughtier and cheerful after the pronouncement of the death sentence. Maintaining his zeal, he waited for the final moment with eagerness. He used to tell his colleagues, "Our journey will end in a flash, the moment we are hanged, but you people are destined to suffer the hardships of the journey for many years. I feel sorry for you all." These words could be told by a man of great poise and composure.

On 18th March 1931, the black warrant issued by the Home Department for the execution of the order of death sentence of Bhagat Singh, Rajguru and Sukhdev was received.

Mother Parvati Devi was informed that her final meeting with Rajguru had been fixed on 23rd March 1931 at 11 a.m. Sardar Kishan Singh, too, received a letter bearing the similar message. He intimated Gandhiji by telegram about this. He also disclosed the letter to newspaper and the news appeared on 20th March 1931 issue of *The Tribune*.

What an irony it was that on one side, the whole nation was mournful on sighting the imminent martyrdom and on the other side, Lord Irwin, who was to be relieved from the post of Viceroy on 15th April, had arranged a grand farewell dinner at Viceroy House on 22nd March 1931 evening.

Taking the flame forward

23rd March 1931

The entire Lahore city was veiled in the thick clouds of suspense and apprehension. The Central Jail had been converted into highest security area and all high officials were present inside. A restless heavy crowd had already gathered outside the Jail by 10 a.m.

Though the hanging had been scheduled on 24th March, 1931 at 7 a.m., but the Government was finding the few remaining hours quite stressful, due to ever-increasing nation-wide public unrest. The signals about advancing the time of execution had already begun to emerge.

The so called peace-loving and judicious Government behaved like a dictator on that day. The first blow had already been delivered by refusing the relatives of three martyrs to have the last meeting with their beloved ones. In protest, many telegrams were sent to Viceroy and Home Member and all Lahore officers were called by phone. But all proved in vain. Finally, the lion-hearted mothers declined to press for the meeting.

Bhagat Singh, Rajguru and Sukhdev were hanged at 7.33 p.m. amidst deafening shouts of patriotic slogans, both from inside and outside the Jail. The light of their life was extinguished, but their sacrifice ignited the torch of freedom.

Such was the atmosphere inside the Jail that an emotionally charged Indian officer declined to identify the deceased. He was immediately terminated from the service and taken in custody. Jail Superintendent, along with two British officers, completed the formalities.

At the same time, Sardar Kishan Singh was addressing a large gathering at Mori gate, a short while away from the Central Jail. He was given this heart breaking news in the middle of the speech. Without betraying any emotions, he continued his speech and kept the crowd under control. When he, followed by the large crowd, reached the Jail to collect the bodies, the gates were not opened. The tyrannical officials had cut the bodies into multiple pieces, packed in the bags, secretly loaded in trucks standing at the rear gate and transported to unknown destination.

The truck took a Hindu Pundit and Sikh priest from Kasoor and then reached Post no. 201 near *Kesar-e-Hind* Bridge, *Hussaniwala*, a short distance away from Ferozepur. The soldiers, at the banks of River Satluj, unloaded the sacks, poured kerosene oil over the body pieces and set them on fire. Seeing the flames, thousands of persons from Ferozepur searching for the bodies, dashed to the spot at once. The frightened soldiers extinguished the fire, threw the remaining mortal remains in the flowing water, covered the place with sand and escaped. Only some of the remains could be recovered after intense search in the morning.

The pieces were not distinguishable from each other. They were taken to the banks of river Ravi at Lahore and cremated before a funeral procession of nearly one lakh people.

That was the second insult the Government had attempted to inflict on the national pride by mutilating the bodies of the martyrs. The tales of these immortals ignited the public mind so much, that everybody resolved to become independent and throw the cruel British out. Their dream of independence finally became a reality 17 years later on 15th August 1947, when Indian tricolour replaced Union Jack in the Indian skies.

Appendix-I

Family tree of Shivram Hari Rajguru

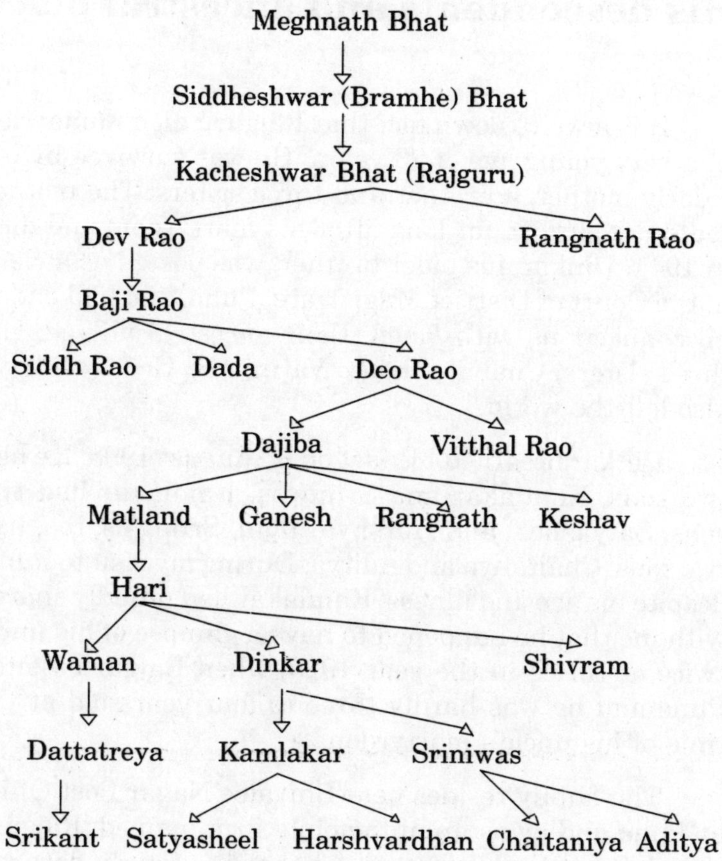

Appendix-II

His descendents and ancestral place

It is a well known fact that Rajguru died unmarried at a very young age of 23 years. He was survived by his elderly mother, a brother and three sisters. The mother could not survive for long after his martyrdom and died in 1941. Dinkar, his elder brother, was posted as a clerk in the Court of District Magistrate, Pune, and had ended all connections with Khed, their ancestral village. His three sisters, Chandrabhaga, Varini and Godavari have also left the world.

Dinkar breathed his last on 6th August 1998. He had two sons, Kamlakar and Sriniwas. Kamlakar had two sons, Satyasheel and Harshvardhan. Sriniwas, too, had two sons, Chaitanya and Aditya. During my visit to Pune, despite his age and illness, Kamlakar had proudly shared with me that he happened to have a glimpse of his uncle twice or thrice in the year 1929, when Rajguru visited Pune and he was hardly three to four years old at the time of his uncle's martyrdom.

The family resides near Shivajee Nagar Post Office at Pune and owns an automobile firm, named 'Rajguru Sales'. Sayasheel informed me that the family does not own any object, reminiscent of his uncle.

Indeed no sincere effort has been made to treasure the memories of the departed soul in a museum anywhere in India. A pen belonging to Rajguru donated on 29th December 1995 by Rajyam Sinha, wife of his colleague, Vijay Kumar Sinha is available at Tilak Museum. Pune. The museum also displays two letters written in Marathi by Rajguru. Nobody is aware of the metal box, which was seized from him at the time of his arrest.

Film industry has produced six movies on Bhagat Singh, his colleague, but despite National Film Institute being located in Pune, no one has come forward to produce a film on this great martyr.

There have been many instances when people, jailed for petty crimes, have obtained false certificates verifying imprisonment as freedom fighters and obtained financial and other benefits. The great martyr's family has, however, never received any such benefits.

It is an irony that we, even after so many years of becoming independent, are not able to pay due respect to our martyrs, which they deserved, while those supporting and obeying the tyrannical British Government, have flourished. Hansraj Vohra, the traitor-turned-approver, was rewarded with the facility of higher education at London. Veerbhadra Tiwari, the person responsible for Azad's martyrdom, was provided with a bodyguard, apart from a cash award of Rs. 15000. This was not enough. Post-independence, he managed to become the Block President in Orai (UP). Inspector Shambhunath, for his gun battle with Azad, was awarded with honorific titles of Rai Bahadur and M.B.E. while, Jagrani Devi, Azad's mother, was left among tribal people to survive in unhygienic circumstances and died in the year 1951 in a state of great poverty. Is this the respect, we have reserved for these great sons of the nation?

Khed, the birth place of Rajguru, is located 45 kilometers (26 miles) away from Pune on Pune-Nasik highway. The Maharashtra Government, to commemorate the lasting memory of the great son of the land, has renamed it "RAJGURUNAGAR", about 30 years back. The village was known in ancient times as "Khetak" and was a place of great pilgrimage.

A golden colored statue of Rajguru, placed under a red coloured umbrella, has been erected in the front of the bus stand on the side of Highway. This was unveiled on 6th May 1978, by Yashvant Rao Chavan, the then Defence Minister, in presence of Vasant Rao Patil, the then Chief Minister of Maharashtra. A college is located at a little distance. Within its vast premises, a monument in his name has been erected, where the students regularly pay their homage.

The actual place of his birth is called "Rajgurubada", located at a height on the banks of river Bheema. Rajguru, along with his family members, lived here in two rooms and a verandah, located on river side of the building. The building now is in quite a miserable condition, but still, 15 to 20 middle class families are residing here . The Government, to build a national monument, has issued them with notices to vacate this place and occupy alternative facility, but they have not shifted as yet. Sardar Kultar Singh, Bhagat Singh's brother, during his visit, felt quite distressed at the pitiable sight of the place.

Indian Archeological Survey is supervising the construction activities of the structure, but the decorum and grandeur of a national level are missing. The area of construction is too small and the construction job has been delegated to unskilled persons. The place is surrounded by trespassers and the connecting path to main road is also quite tedious. The persons in the neighbourhood are also quite disinterested, as they fear imminent migration.

Though there are many grand modern buildings and complexes in Rajguru Nagar, but no body, including the government, local residents or even his descendents, seem bothered about preserving the pious memory of the great martyr. I often wonder: will history excuse them for the exhibition of this degree of insensitiveness in this modern era!

Appendix-III

Letter to his brother (in Marathi)

Borstal Jail, Lahore "Shri Kacheshwar Sharanam"

March 10th 1930

Loving regards. This is to mention I have not, since your departure, received any letter intimating your reaching back home. There was only a letter about reaching at the address of Mr. Bhatwadekar. I fail to understand as to why there has been no letter after that and why such a thing is happening. Anyway, my health has improved and I have stopped taking medicines. Likewise, I have also started eating light food. We all play volleyball, in the evening. I participated for a shortwhile yesterday as well today evening, but started feeling weak soon. Similary, many a times, I face problems, while playing, due to lack of flexibility in the body, but the health is getting better every day. Four days back, I weighed 102 pounds while prior to illness my weight was 105 pounds. I have not been weighed after falling sick. However, I hope to recover after significant bed rest, then only recording weight would be advisable. My initial weight, though, was 126 pounds and I will keep you apprised about my latest weight. Do not worry about me. Saturday, I was visited by Mrs. Yamutai, Mr. Baburao and Mr. G.B. Matoshri

Your's

Sd/-

(Shivram Hari Rajguru)

To,

Mr. R.R. Dinkar Hari Rajguru

460, Narain Peth, Poona, Poona City

Appendix-IV

Second letter to his brother (In Marathi)

Borstal Jail, Lahore   March 10th 1930

Loving regards. It is really surprising not to have received any communication. The letters from our relatives are one of the sources to keep us apprised as to what is happening outside. The letters are regularly scanned here and are, at times, handed to us after removing the objectionable contents. At times, letters are even forefeited. Your letters have minimum of this type of contents, and, therefore, there is least chance of any disturbance. We get the outside news usually through newspapers and relatives of other colleagues. Even then, I am always curious to learn more news from Maharashtra, as we are neither permitted nor supplied with the Maharashtra newspapers. The newspapers here make very little mention about the events there. If we leave this too apart, but one always longs to learn the opinions and whereabouts of his near and dear ones. The reading of a letter gives the same amount of joy as that provided by a meeting.

My health is improving. As far as I remember, my face never looked so weak in the past. After the hunger strike, taking care of health has led to physical improvement, but restoration of power to the previous levels will take sometime. At the beginning of the strike, I had craving for food for first three to four days. On feeling hunger, we consume plain water. We take that even in scant quantity, and I myself consume only one cup of water in two days at times. Less or no consumption of water leads to dehydration, weakness, bad taste and smell in the mouth, which does not improve even after gargling two to three times. At times, breathing quickens up or slows down. Due to weakness, the support becomes necessary during walking. All this is caused by water deprivation. It is almost impossible to give up drinking water absolutely. (...... No clearly legible ....) I did not take water for four days, just kept my lips wet. It is quite natural to fall after observing fast at this level for seven to eight days. Later recovery of health was attempted by giving milk and water, but even then, I suffered from fever and may as well have pneumonia too.

Respected mother should be about to reach Pune. I am well here and will feel better in next two to three days. Please convey my respectful regards to *Bhabhiji* and other elders and love to beloved Godu, Gopal and Kamlakar.

Your's

Sd/-

(Shivram Hari Rajguru)

Appendix-V

Letter to the Governor of Punjab

March 20th 1931

Shimla

To

Governor

Punjab

Sir,

With due respect we beg to bring to your kind notice the following:

That we were sentenced to death on 7th October 1930 by a British Court, L.C.C. Tribunal, constituted under the Sp. Lahore Conspiracy Case Ordinance, Promulgated by H.E. The Viceroy, the Head of the British Government of India, and that the main charge against us was that of having waged war against H.M. King George, the King of England.

The above-mentioned finding of the Court presupposed two things:

Firstly, that there exists a state of war between the British nation and the Indian nation and, secondly, that we had actually participated in that war and were therefore war prisoners.

The second pre-supposition seems to be a little bit flattering, but nevertheless it is too tempting to resist the desire of acquiescence in it. As regards the first, we are constrained to go into some detail. Apparently, there seems to be no such war as the phrase indicates. Nevertheless, please allow us to accept the validity of the pre-supposition taking it at its face value. But in order to be correctly understood, we must explain it further. Let us declare that the state of war does exist and shall exist so long as the Indian toiling masses and the natural resources are being exploited by a handful of parasites. They may be purely British capitalist or mixed British and Indian or even purely Indian. They may be carrying on their insidious exploitation through mixed or even on purely Indian bureaucratic apparatus. All these things make no difference. No matter, if your Government tries and succeeds in winning over the leaders of the upper strata of the Indian society through petty concessions and compromises and thereby cause a temporary demoralization in the main body of the forces. No matter, if once again the vanguard of the Indian movement, the Revolutionary Party, finds itself deserted in the thick of the war. No matter if the leaders to whom personally we are much indebted for the sympathy and feelings they expressed for us, but nevertheless we cannot overlook the fact that they did become so callous as to ignore and not to make a mention in the peace negotiation of even the homeless, friendless and penniless female workers who are alleged to be belonging to the vanguard and whom the leaders consider to be enemies of their utopian non-violent cult which has already become a thing of the past; the heroines who had ungrudgingly sacrificed or offered for sacrifice their husbands, brothers, and all that were nearest and dearest to them, including themselves, whom your government has declared to be outlaws. No matter, if your agents stoop so low as to fabricate baseless calumnies against their spotless characters to damage their and their party's reputation. The war shall continue.

It may assume different shapes at different times. It may become now open, now hidden, now purely agitational, now fierce life and death struggle. The choice of the course, whether bloody or comparatively peaceful, which it should adopt, rests with you. Choose whichever you like but that war shall be incessantly waged without taking into consideration the petty (illegible) and the meaningless ethical ideologies. It shall be waged ever with new vigour, greater audacity and unflinching determination till the Socialist Republic is established and the present social order is completely replaced by a new social order, based on social prosperity and thus every sort of exploitation is put an end to and the humanity is ushered into the era of genuine and permanent peace. In the very near future, the final battle shall be fought and final settlement arrived at.

The days of capitalist and imperialist exploitation are numbered. The war neither began with us nor is it going to end with our lives. It is the inevitable consequence of the historic events and the existing environment. Our humble sacrifices shall be only a link in the chain that has very accurately been beautified by the unparalleled sacrifice of Mr. Das and most tragic but noblest sacrifice of comrade Bhagawati Charan and the glorious death of our dear warrior Azad.

As to the question of our fate, please allow us to say that when you have decided to put us to death, you will certainly do it. You have got the power in your hands and the power is the greatest justification in this world. We know that the maxim "Might is right" serves as your guiding motto. The whole of our trial was just a proof of that. We wanted to point out that according to the verdict at your court we had waged war and were therefore war prisoners. And we, claim to be treated as such i.e., we claim, to be shot dead instead to be hanged. It rests with you to prove that you really meant what your court has said.

We request and hope that you will very kindly order the military department to send its detachment to perform our execution.

Yours

Bhagat Singh
Rajguru
Sukhdev

Appendix-VI

Story of J.C. Scott

The history would always register the Saunders' assassination as a symbol of degree of rage and zeal exhibited by revolutionaries to avenge the national insult. But, it would also be remembered that the revolutionaries actually intended to assassinate J.C. Scott, S.S.P., Lahore, who had actually ordered the ill-fated lathi charge, but they ended up killing Saunders, who had delivered the fatal blow to Lalaji. Though he accidentally received the punishment for his foul deed, but one always wonders as to what happened to J.C. Scott after this incident. Let us have the first hand researched information on Scott:

Scott was born at Lancaster City (England) on December 2nd, 1885. He joined Indian Police Services on November 20th, 1915 and was allocated to Joint Punjab Cadre. He was first posted at Multan, and then at Jhang in 1920, as Additional S.P. Thereafter, he served as Superintendent of Police at Miyanwali and Jhelum. He was, then, posted as Senior S.P. of Lahore in the summer of 1926.

He was present, with his police force, at Lahore Railway Station on October 30th, 1928, when Lala Lajpat Rai led a huge procession to boycott Simon Commission.

He ordered his subordinates for lathi charge. Following these orders, Saunders, Additional S.P., Sayyed Ahmed Shah and Niaz Ahmed, both D.S.P., and Ayaz Hussain, Sub-inspector, so brutally assaulted Lalaji and the mob, that Lalaji was badly wounded and finally succumbed to the injuries, one month later.

Azad, Bhagat Singh, Rajguru and Jai Gopal planned to avenge the death of Lalaji. On 17th December 1928, outside Scott's office, they shot Saunders, as Jai Gopal took Saunders for Scott and made the wrong signal.

Constable Abdul Waheed, Scott's Driver (PW 80) deposed before the Lahore Conspiracy Case Tribunal that on 17th December, he had taken Scott to Kasoor at 9.30 a.m., after the breakfast and they had come back at 5.30 p.m. Then, he had left Scott at Sunny View Hotel, where he resided. According to another story, Scott, after receiving a call from his wife, had left the office, riding on a bicycle, as his mother-in-law was expected to come from England. His car, numbered PB-6728 was recognized by everyone at Lahore and he was not averse to the use of jeep, motorcycle and cycle.

He had another escape on January 1st, 1929, while travelling by car near Canal Bridge on Ferozepur road. Sukhdev and Jai Gopal had him well targeted, but Sukhdev refused to shoot him by saying that when he had been saved through luck once, why we should attempt again.

After this episode, fearing another attempt on his life, he was posted as S.S.P., Rawalpindi, replaced by G.T.H. Hardings. He was quite interested in wrestling and boxing and helped to organize many wrestling championships in his career spanning 32 years. He was D.I.G., Lahore range, at the time of freedom of India. He applied for continuing services in independent India, but was refused by Indian Government on account of the blemish of Lalaji's death.

He returned to England after retirement and breathed his last in Osborn County. He was survived by Dorothy, his wife and two married daughters. He will always remain an inseparable part of Indian freedom struggle history for his haunted deeds.

Appendix-VII

Central Jail, Lahore - then and now

The Central Jail, Lahore, where Bhagat Singh, Rajguru and Sukhdev were martyred on March 23rd, 1931, has been reduced to vestiges. The cells housing the brave youth are now in wrecks.

The martyrs, belonging to the era of undivided India, are now least remembered in the city, where they spent their last days fighting the tyrannical British. Those freedom fanatics had never imagined that India would be partitioned in two parts and they would not be given the recognition which they deserved. Of late, the mindsets have changed and more and more people are willing to recognize these great sons as their own.

Peace still abounds on the tree lined Jail Road, an excursion from the Temple Road in Lahore. Moving towards Gulmarg, one can still observe the relics of a clay wall of the jail, at one time the site of residential quarters for the jail employees. Near to it, was located the scaffold, where the trio was hanged. Instead of a monumnet, this place is represented by a traffic post, around which the clouds of dust and smoke totally obscure the glorious reminiscences of the past.

At one time, the area of the jail was so large that the officials were required to use a cart to move from one corner to another. Regretfully, only a wall remains of that site as most of the remnants were demolished about ten years back, under political pressure, to create the space for a residential colony. Though no body dared to purchase the place of hanging, locally known as *Phansighat*, believing it as the abode of souls, but later the greed prevailed over the fear and this, too, was sold.

The gates used by the Jailors and the rear gate have all become non-existent. The costliest and grandest colony of Lahore, called Shadman Colony, is located here. Not even a single pillar has been erected to commemorate the memory of the martyrs. Though of late, the Pakistan Government has announced to construct a monument at this site, but the implementation is long awaited.

The Government of India requested the Government of Pakistan, after the partition, to return the records of the Lahore Conspiracy Case, Jail records and personal belongings of the martyrs. After a long delay, the Pakistan Government replied in negation, stating that all the articles have already been destroyed.

Mr. D.P. Yadav, M.P., raised the following questions to be answered by Minister of State for External Affairs, numbered 954, in the Rajya Sabha on July 26th 2002:

a. Has the Government made the demands for return of the clothes of martyrs Bhagat Singh, Sukhdev and Rajguru from the officials of the Lahore Jail?

b. Knowing that these martyrs are worshipped by the millions, what are the reasons for non-procurement of the clothes last worn by them from the Lahore Jail.

Mr. Digvijay Singh, Minister of State for External affairs, informed the House in affirmative. He said that the Government of India had requested the Government of Pakistan to return the clothes and personal belongings of the martyrs, but the corresponding officers from Pakistan have informed that the articles were not found as all the records and articles in the jail have been destroyed.

Recently, Jag Mohan Singh, the nephew of Bhagat Singh had informed me that 175 books belonging to Bhagat Singh, which were seized from the headquarters of Hindustan Socialist Republication Army at Nai ki Mandi, Agra in 1929, are still lying in shabby state in lower courts in Lahore.

Appendix-VIII

Hussainiwala - Salute to Martyrs

Bhagat Singh, Sukhdev and Rajguru were always a prickly thorn in the bed of the British Government, who could never be plucked off during their life. The British could never be at ease even after mutilating and burning their mortal remains. This blemish on the forehead of so-called gentlemen community will stay forever. But the land, where these mortal remains fell, turned sanctimonious.

Bhagat Singh, Sukhdev and Rajguru were executed a day earlier than the hanging scheduled in the Central Jail Lahore at 7.33 p.m., on March 23, 1931. The entire city of Lahore was in the grip of national fervour and there were apprehensions of revolt. The Jail authorities broke the back wall of the Jail and secretly brought the dead bodies of the martyrs on the banks of river Satluj near Ferozepur for an unceremonial cremation. When the local people, at visulizing the flames, moved towards them, they put out the fire, threw unburnt remains in the river, covered the place with sand and escaped. The local peasants cordoned that area with bamboos and wooden logs. Next day, Noujawan Bharat Sabha, passed a resolution to construct a memorial here but terrified British demolished that area. They could never imagine that the site would one day become a national treasure.

With the passage of time, the efforts of all freedom fighters resulted in independence of India on 15th August 1947. But, the cunning British succeeded in securing the partition of India on religious basis. They did to India what they had done to the bodies of the martyrs about 17 years back. The sanctity of the land was breached by the assaults and rapes resulting in innumerable corpses of the children, females, elderly and innocent people. The colourless water turned red. This was not what our martyrs had in their vision.

Most unfortunately, the line of partition traversed through this pious land. The cremation site went inside Pakistan's control, thus depriving every Indian his right to pay homage.

In January 1961, this piece of land once again came within Indian border when untiring efforts of the Indian Government ended in exchange of lands by way of adjustment. Since then, this deserted place, 300 meters away from the border and spanning a few square meters only, has become a national heritage. Hussainiwala is a border village on banks of River Sutlej in Forezepur district of Punjab State. The place is named after Peer Baba Hussainiwala ji (Saint who is of Husain.") It is under control of Indian military and is visited by thousands of tourists.

In the same year, a fair was organized to celebrate the 30th anniversary of their martyrdom, which was attended by visitors from all over the nation. The fair is now being organized customarily every year. At the same time, a rock was placed over a brick platform, which had the faces of the three martyrs inscribed on it. One can also visualize a pillar, made up of red bricks, among the weeds near the deserted railway line, which has bore testimony to several frightening sights.

The Chief Minister of Punjab, during his visit in September 1964, made a declaration regarding the construction of a memorial with contribution from the government as well as the public, conforming to the grace of the martyrs. A total of Rs. 65,000 was raised, the government contributing Rs. 5,000. The foundation was laid, after offering of the flowers, by Yashwant Rao Chavan, the then Defence Minister of India, on March 23rd. 1965. This time a graceful monument was erected. It is also the cremation place of Batukeshwar Dutta, a close aide of Bhagat Singh, who died in 1965. His last wish was to cremate him at the place where Bhagat Singh, Rajguru and Sukhdev were cremated.

Punjab Government, respecting the public sentiments, started the construction of a grand memorial in February 1968, which was completed within a short time at a cost of Rs. 1.85 Lakh. The memorial was in the form of 152 feet long and 104 feet wide clear water filled pond, surrounded by 16 feet wide circumambulation path. In the centre of the pond, an octagonal black stone, surrounded by 8 feet wide circumambulation path, symbolized the blemish committed by the British. The approach road was 88 feet long and 8 feet wide.

The memorial was pledged to the nation on March 23rd, 1968, exactly 37 years after their martyrdom, by Sardar Laxman Singh Gill, the Chief Minister of Punjab, who unveiled the bronze statues of late Bhagat Singh, Sukhdev and Rajguru. The event was made more significant by the thousands of visitors, who had come here to witness this historic moment.

The emotions arose, when 86 years old Mother Vidyawati, the mother of Bhagat Singh, arrived on the stage. Everybody stood up in her respect. She first moved towards the memorial, showered the flowers and bowed before and circumambulated around the statues of her brave sons. She, instead of being recipient of the respect from her sons, was paying respect to them instead as they, now, being the martyrs, deserved to be respected by everyone.

Kiran Chandra, brother of another great martyr, Yateendranath Das delivered a brilliant speech, which left the audience spellbound. More was yet to come. Godavri, Rajguru's sister, clad in Maharashtrian attire, climbed up the stage and landed in great mother's arm. Their tears were telling the entire story. They soon landed in the memories of past when 37 years back, Godavari, along with her mother, had travelled from Pune to Lahore, just nine days prior to hanging and stayed with Bhagat Singh's family.

Only three years later, India and Pakistan engaged in fierce battle. In the fight, 15 Punjab's two companies were attacked on Indian side by four brigades of the Pakistan Army, including 5000 Pakistani army men along with 15 tanks and heavy artillery support at 1835 hours on 2nd December 1971. Despite being in a lesser strength, Maj. S.P.L. Waraich and Maj. Singh's companies fought with the enemy gallantly on the midnight of 2nd, 3rd December, 1971 and succeeded in putting restraint on Pakistani army. The officers were later decorated with *Param Vishisht Seva Medal.*

Once again, the sacred place witnessed the dreadful sight of massive bloodshed between two countries. Unfortunately, lots of memorials were destroyed by heavy artillery firing of Pakistan army, the marks of which can still be observed even today.

In 1973, The Government of India erected a new memorial at the same site to honour the loving memory of the martyrs.

On June 1st, 1975, Mother Vidyawati, too, left the world to rest in peace with her beloved sons. She was also cremated there as per her last wish and later she was awarded with title of '*Punjab Mata*' i.e. Mother of Punjab.

Prakash Singh Badal, the Chief Minister of Punjab has made the announcement on 23rd March 2008, that a tourist hub shall be developed near the Hussainiwala Memorial at a cost of Rs. ten million. Every day, by means of a light and sound program, the tourists shall be made aware of the life of Bhagat Singh, Sukhdev, Rajguru and Lala Lajpat Rai. The road from Firozepur Cantt. to the International Border shall also be decorated with lights.

The headquarters of Border Security Force (B.S.F.) is located at Hussainiwala border of India-Pakistan. A memorial to commemorate the memory of martyrs of 1971 war has been constructed. Like Wagah border, every day between 6.00 p.m.-6.30 p.m. guards of both the sides, jointly perform a ceremony called lowering of the flags'. It may seem slightly aggressive, but it really is just entertainment for the crowds from both sides.

I had the fortune to visit Hussainiwala and pay homage to the martyrs at the memorial. The sight of Indian tricolor and green Pakistani flag on either sides of the border, showing the two parts of our beloved nation, raised my emotions. This is not what our great ancestors had struggled for. Will the two nations join together again, like two factions of Germany?

References

1. '*Yugdrashta Bhagat Singh Aur Unke Mrityunjaya Purkhe*' by Veerendra Sindhu, Edtn. 1997, Rajpal and Sons, Delhi.
2. '*Amar Shaheed Bhagat Singh*' by Jitendra Nath Sanyal, Edtn. 1999, National Book Trust of India, New Delhi.
3. '*Shaheed Bhagat Singh: Kranti Mein Ek Prayog*' by Kuldeep Nair, Edtn. 2001, Diamond Pocket Books. Delhi.
4. '*Yash Ki Dharohar*' by Bhagwan Das Mahore, Sadashiv and Shiv Verma, Edtn. 1988, Atmaram and Sons, Delhi
5. '*Mere Bhai Shaheed Sukhdev*' by Mathuradas Thapar, Edtn. 1992. *Shaheed Smark Prakashan*, Delhi
6. '*Sansmratiyan*' by Shiv Verma, Edtn. 1991, Shaheed Smarak Prakashan, Lucknow
7. '*Krantikarak Rajguru*' (Marathi) by Dr. Sachchidanand Shewde Edtn. 2007, *Nav Chaitanya Prakashan, Mumbai.*
8. '*Hutatma Shivram Rajguru*' (Marathi) by Deepakant Rakshe, Edtn. 1999, Hutatma Rajguru Prakashan Samiti, Maharashtra
9. '*Bhagat Singh Ke Sampoorna Dastavej*' by Chamanlal, Adhaar Prakashan, Haryana

10. '*Bhagat Singh Ke Pata Aur Dastavej*' by Veerendra Sandhu, Edtn. 1996, Rajpal and Sons, Delhi.

11. '*Kranti Murti Durga Bhabhi*' by Vachnesh Tripathi. Edtn. 1996, Hindi Academy, Delhi.

12. '*Krantikari Shaheed Rajguru*' by Shri Krishna Saral, Edtn. 1995, Rashtriya Prakashan, Ujjain (MP)

13. '*Sardar Bhagat Singh Aur Unke Saathi*' by Ajay Kumar Ghosh, Edtn. 2005, Navodaya Sales, New Delhi.

14. '*Bhagat Singh Aur Swatantrata Sangram*' by Dr. Raghubeer Singh, Radha Publications, New Delhi

15. '*Chandra Shekhar Azad*' by Manmath Nath Gupt, Edtn. 1972, Hind Pocket Books Pvt. Ltd., Delhi

16. '*Amar Shaheed Bhagat Singh*' by Vishnoo Prabhakar, Edtn. 1976, Hind Pocket Books Pvt Ltd., Delhi.

17. '*The Trial of Bhagat Singh*' (English) by A. G. Noorani, Edtn. 1996, Konark Prakashan Pvt. Ltd., Delhi

18. '*Bandi Jeevan*' by Shacheendra Nath Sanyal

19. '*Bharat Ke Krantiveer*' by Dr. Tara Chandra Pal Baikal, Edtn. 2002, Dynamic Publications India Ltd., Merut (UP).

20. '*Krantiveer Chandra Shekhar Azad*' by Dr. Lal Bahadur Singh, Edtn. 2000, Swastik Prakashan, Delhi

21. '*Bhagat Singh: The Eternal Rebel*' by Malwinder Jeet Singh Waraich, Edtn. 2007, Publications Division, Ministry of Information and Broadcasting Government of India, New Delhi.